T0002806

The Practice
of the
Presence of
Jesus

The Practice of the Presence of Jesus

Daily Meditations on the Nearness of Our Savior

Joni Eareckson Tada

with John Sloan

MULTNOMAH

FOR JOHN SLOAN

*Is there an editor who loves books as much
as you? Maybe. But surely, there's no editor
who loves their authors more than you.
And for that I am grateful to God.*

Contents

Introduction

About Brother Lawrence

Brother Lawrence never intended for his letters to be read around the world. A monk who lived hundreds of years ago, he is best known today as the author of *The Practice of the Presence of God*. His book is small enough to fit in one hand and short enough to read in a day. But it has tremendous implications for anyone who picks it up. It became a phenomenal classic that has sold millions of copies in the last five decades. This little book of Lawrence's letters and conversations was not even credited to him initially; Lawrence never got to see his influence, but that would not have mattered to him.

Brother Lawrence was a monk, a soldier, a peasant servant, a mystic, and a man who sought God for many years. He was born Nicholas Herman to peasant parents in eastern France in 1608 or 1614 (the date of his birth is uncertain).

Europe's Thirty Years' War raged around Lawrence as he grew up. His childhood was marked by the conflict, and he entered military service young. His soldier's wages paid for a small amount of food daily. He was on the battlefield against the French, Germans, Swedes, and other nations in a horrific, pugilistic war. It was the brutality of personal combat in the war that bothered Lawrence, not the politics.

All the earth ... is at rest.
Zech. 1:11

He was also known for his bravery in that war. During one engagement, a party of German troops took him prisoner. They declared him a spy and treated him as such; they threatened to hang him. But he told them he wasn't frightened in the least, he wasn't who they stated he was, and therefore his conscience led him to look upon death indifferently. His honesty floored them, and the German officers let him go.

While a soldier, he had an experience that deepened his spiritual life. One winter, he saw a barren tree without leaves and fruit. He realized that he was like the barren tree—he would be transformed through God's power but only after a long season of very little fruit.

A blow ended Lawrence's service. He received a leg wound so grievous and deep that he no longer walked like a man untouched by war. He was set aside like an old piece of furniture, never to be used again. His injury later led to "sciatic gout" (known today as arthritis of the hip joint) and an ulcerated wound, which caused a distinct limp. He couldn't escape some feelings of bitterness, but in his later writings he asserted the providence and care of God in war. Even in the face of life-changing afflictions, Lawrence admonished others to hope: "Hope in Him more than ever: thank Him with me for the favours He does you, particularly for the fortitude and patience which He gives you in your afflictions: it is a plain mark of the care He takes of you; comfort yourself then with Him, and give thanks for all."

No longer able to serve as a soldier, he searched for another line of employment. He found work as a footman, opening carriage step-downs for the elite after their travels in the coach. Yet he proved incompetent at his job. Later he would claim that he broke everything he touched—the steps or pieces of a coach and presumably the livery of his coachman's customers. It was another training ground for his later spirituality, but he would not linger there for long.

A broken soldier and hopeless footman, Lawrence decided to turn to a religious life. He joined the Discalced Carmelite monastery in Paris. Lawrence was unchanged by his seminary life for his first decade there. He performed his tasks—washing dishes, carrying pots and pans, lifting hot kettles of scalding water, or cooking meals in the deep pans he later scrubbed. He mopped and swept floors. He was still clumsy.

But it was there in the scullery that he found his secret: practicing the presence of God. He described the moment like this: "I was troubled sometimes with thoughts . . . that there was no salvation for me. When I thought of nothing but to end my days in these troubles. . . . I found myself changed all at once; and my soul, which, till that time, was in trouble, felt a profound inward peace, as if she were in her centre and place of rest."

Brother Lawrence realized that God was always with him, even during the most menial tasks. And just by acknowledging God's presence, the most mundane jobs and the bleakest surroundings could be filled with God's love and light.

Brother Lawrence devoted himself completely to practicing God's presence everywhere.

God blessed Lawrence in the kitchen and in the chapel, in times of pleasantness and in times of affliction, in whatever circumstances were brought his way. While others would rush to complete their duties, Brother Lawrence would do the same work, and more, but he was ever mindful that God was present. There was no need to rush away from the presence of God. Lawrence had conversations with God while he worked, and his simple life was replete with satisfaction. As he wrote, "There is not in the world a kind of life more sweet and delightful, than that of a continual conversation with GOD."

Through his awareness of his Father's presence beside him, Lawrence walked intimately with God through the remaining days of his life, each year becoming closer and closer to the One he served. Lawrence realized that even his mistakes were inroads to deeper communion with God: "I was very aware of my faults, but not discouraged by them. I confessed them to God and did not excuse myself. When I had done so, I peaceably resumed my usual practice of love and adoration." His lifelong pursuit of God was realized, and his practice of the presence of God was recorded in letters and conversations.

Brother Lawrence found a desire for God that eliminated all other passions: "Let all our employment be to *know* GOD: the more one *knows* Him, the more one desires to *know* Him." He conversed with God in as familiar a way as with any other soul upon the earth. The monk humbly recommended his practice to others, knowing that the presence of God could be revealed to anyone who desired to know him better: "Were I a preacher, I should above all other things preach the practice of *the presence of* GOD; and, were I a director, I should advise all the world to it: so necessary do I think it, and so easy too."

Lawrence discovered a secret that is simple and true, and yet takes a lifetime to put into practice. He found that in our own lives, we can live every day, every hour, and every moment in the presence of God. We can, like Lawrence, be in the middle of pots and pans, and yet be experiencing God's presence. That's what mattered the most to Lawrence—finding God in every present moment. He would want all of us to experience that grace.[1]

About Joni Eareckson Tada

Joni Eareckson grew up in the era of new appliances, toasters, televisions, and two-car garages, where homes looked much the same on each block. In many 1950s post-war homes, church and Sunday school were routine for American families. Although conversations with her sisters and parents were laced with references to God and the Bible, Joni's awareness of Jesus was more connected to his teachings than his nearness. The Bible enjoyed a prominent place in the living room but was revered from a distance.

The Earecksons' faithfulness was most evident in their daily singing. They knew countless Christian hymns and regularly sang together. It was not considered odd to break into a hymn while doing chores, yard work, sitting around the table after dessert, or heading up the stairs for bed. The words of hymns shaped Joni's early spiritual life:

My hope is built on nothing less
than Jesus' blood and righteousness;
I dare not trust the sweetest frame,
but wholly lean on Jesus' name.[2]

The name of Jesus remained familiar on the lips of Joni and her sisters.

The Eareckson family had roots extending back to the beginnings of the Reformed Episcopal Church, a small conservative and liturgical denomination. In the Eareckson household, the King James edition of the *Book of Common Prayer* stood opened; Joni learned many psalms by heart. She also learned the Collect for Purity, the Nicene and Apostles' Creeds, the General Thanksgiving, the Confession of Sin, and other prayers. She felt more comfortable with the rhythms of liturgy than the free-form services of most evangelical churches that her friends attended.

The last of four girls, Joni struggled to keep up with her active family who thought nothing of closing up the house for the summer to tent camp among the sand dunes of the Delaware shore. Joni would lie on the beach at night, harmonizing with her sisters, who all knew countless gospel songs by heart. Under the stars she sensed another song, rhythmic like ocean waves, resonating with hints of God's immense presence far above her. She later described how she felt her first strong stirrings of the Spirit and a deep longing to know him better while beach camping—there had to be more to Jesus than what was lauded of God in songs and in her prayer book.

As a high school sophomore, fifteen-year-old Joni found herself captivated by the gospel presentation she heard at Young Life, an evangelistic outreach on her high school campus. Sitting cross-legged on the floors of local gathering spots like churches and homes, she sensed for the first time that Jesus—the Jesus her family had sung about, the Christ that her prayer book celebrated, the Almighty God who was the focus of Sunday services at her church—was, indeed, *personal*. Through Young Life, Joni became aware that Christ did not die for the general sins of everyone—he died for her. That awareness turned a key, and Joni apprehended her Savior personally. All the liturgy and hymns instantly gelled into a new understanding of Jesus's constant presence.

She immediately enrolled in confirmation classes at the Reformed Episcopal Church. Doctrines of heaven and hell, forgiveness, grace, justification, and sanctification took root quickly. Biblical precepts that once were vague became deeply familiar. She chose Galatians 2:20 as her life verse: "I have been crucified with Christ. It is no longer I who live, but Christ who lives in me. And the life I now live in the flesh I live by faith in the Son of God, who loved me and gave himself for me" (ESV). She would know later what it meant to be "crucified with Christ."

The late 1960s ushered in the sexual revolution, and Joni fell under its influence. During her remaining school years, she lapsed into moral failures that became habitual and dragged her downward into a deep spiritual depression. She longed to follow Christ, but with each sinful and irresponsible choice, she found herself enslaved. Joni wanted to repent but lost her ability to resist temptation. It crushed her to realize she had become a hypocrite—confessing Jesus in the light and denying him in the dark.

Weeks before her high school graduation, knowing that her lifestyle would only get worse on a college campus away from home, Joni prayed an ominous prayer. She boldly pleaded for God to do whatever—absolutely anything—to rescue her from her enslavement to lust. Shortly afterward, she broke her neck.

After her tragic accident, every Christian conviction she had was put to the test. And when the permanency of her paralysis finally hit her, Joni was filled with horror. Romans 8:28, with its assurance that God could work everything into a pattern for good, seemed almost trite as she faced life without use of her hands and legs. She reflected later, "This isn't a boating accident; this is the sinking of the *Titanic*." The hospital warehoused Joni on the geriatric ward of a state institution. Watching her friends head to college, land jobs out of state, or get married only increased her sense of isolation. The ward felt like a prison. A numbing despair crept into her life, along with thoughts of suicide. She violently thrashed her head on her pillow, hoping to break her neck again and end her life.

Joni's older sister Jay saw her sibling spiraling downward. She opened the family farm to Joni. Even with the state institution behind her, Joni's depression lingered. She sat for hours staring out at the farm fields. Friends made phone calls; they weren't answered. Visitors arrived at the door; she stayed in bed. For weeks, Joni remained in a dark room with drapes pulled shut.

Eventually, Joni found the strength to pray, "God, if I can't die, please show me how to live." The next day she rallied, sat up in her wheelchair, and began moving forward into life. The *Book of Common Prayer,* with its Scripture-laced liturgy, was constantly on her lips. Joni began to thrive on the family farm. She found a smile.

Miss Eareckson refused to skate the surface of the questions that plagued her. Her friends—mostly college-aged Calvinists—created a circle of prayer for her. She took part in study sessions that lasted long into the night as friends munched pizza and mulled over difficult questions together. There was always plenty of music, feasting, and games, and there were even midnight hikes along the river that bordered the farm. The gatherings were an epiphany. These personal relationships gave shape to what Christian love should look and feel like.

Books were placed on a music stand, and Joni was able

to flip the pages using a mouth stick. She studied Dr. Lorraine Boettner's *The Reformed Doctrine of Predestination*, a lengthy work that helped her understand the expansive extent of God's sovereignty over all afflictions. She was astounded to learn that the reach of God's dominion covered even the granules of shifting sand below the very waters in which she broke her neck. Far from off-putting, she found the doctrine of God's sovereignty comforting.

She found a friend in Jonathan Edwards and his small book *Heaven: A World of Love*. Through its pages, she learned the connection between a Christian's response to suffering and that suffering's impact for eternity. From Edwards, Joni learned that trusting and obeying God in her afflictions would increase her capacity for joy, worship, and service in heaven. This was a revelation that would forever shape the way she viewed her own suffering. As Edwards wrote, "They that are highest in degree in glory, will be of the highest capacity; and so having the greatest knowledge, will see most of God's loveliness, and consequently will have love to God and love to the saints most abounding in their hearts."[3] Edwards's theology would be a guiding principle for living with paralysis.

Joni's spiritual formation was largely influenced by Puritans and Reformed pastors and theologians, including Elisabeth Elliot, the jungle missionary whose husband was murdered by the indigenous tribe he was seeking to reach. These reformers—and their sturdy, pragmatic approach to experiencing Jesus Christ—provided a safety net for this quadriplegic as she struggled through setbacks with her severe disability. She gravitated to authors and thinkers who wrote out of their own anguish and heartache.

Joni sat on the back porch of the family farm and listened to cassettes of R. C. Sproul and John Gerstner, modern Calvinists who strengthened her positions of the sovereignty of God and his care, even in bad times. Richard Baxter, an English Puritan, helped her manage her wandering emotions. And Thomas Goodwin taught her about the tenderness of Christ in her afflictions. These teachers guided her away from the theological progressivism popular in the 1970s.

Joni found refreshment in the writings and poetry of Catholic mystics Jeanne-Marie Guyon and François Fénelon. Their experiences of suffering and their expressions of Christ's nearness softened her theology. Catholic theologian Dr. Peter Kreeft and his classic, *Making Sense Out of Suffering,* also became a well-worn resource on Joni's bookshelf.

Miss Eareckson became a "five-point Calvinist," a theology known for its strong emphasis on God's sovereignty. The Carmelite monk Brother Lawrence emphasized a person's free will. These two were different theologies, so it was odd that Joni found the humble work of a Carmelite monk meaningful and helpful in her quest for God's peace. Joni had read *The Practice of the Presence of God* shortly after she came to Christ in high school; the book was trending then with young believers. His simple routine of daily knowing, seeing, and apprehending God in his workday habits intrigued her in high school, and now—in the uncluttered routine of living on the family farm—Joni had occasion to revisit his work. She found *The Practice of the Presence of God* winsome, simple, and engaging, which was a refreshing break from her Reformed writers and thinkers.

Joni found Lawrence's thoughts invigorating. He offered a no-nonsense approach to sin and its decaying effects on a lively relationship with God. But because her afflictions continually tested her faith, she would often fall into sin: grumbling that she could not walk, snapping at her sister, or envying others who went on to marry and start families. The writings of the monk gave a ruthless assessment of sin's damaging influence as well as a tender appreciation for God's grace and forgiveness. The seventeenth-century Carmelite's writings touched her deeply.

She was drawn to Lawrence's authenticity. Here was a Christian man who suffered greatly. Like her, he struggled morally and deeply regretted having wandered far from his spiritual moorings. When he failed spiritually, he admitted his sin and was quick to repent. Joni respected that.

Unlike the unpresuming monk, known only for his menial kitchen duties, Joni's renown for her contentment in suffering grew to celebrity status. Her books and the movie produced about her life thrust her onto a global stage. Brother Lawrence's humble posture served as a caution. She was wary of fame's enticements and recognized its only benefit: a wider sphere of influence for Christ. She has kept to this unambitious posture throughout her life.

Over the following decades, Joni would casually flip

through *The Practice of the Presence of God* and be refreshed by Lawrence's noncomplex approach to life and to God. Initially, she was intrigued by his effusiveness over the love and grace of God, as though it were the answer alone to all ailments and evils in the world. It read like spiritual sentimentality. But over time—as she endured much suffering herself—it became clear to Joni that the supreme love of God was, indeed, the answer to the world's tragic predicament.

Lawrence underplayed the redemptive work of Christ as the fullest expression of God's love for a wounded world. Joni recognized this, seeing the difference between her Calvinist theology and his Catholic theology. Still, she found value in Lawrence's call to an uncluttered engagement with God through a daily practice of his presence.

Many far-ranging influences, from Calvinist to Catholic, have contributed to Joni's spiritual formation. Many theological tributaries helped fill the river of this woman's love for Christ, but God's Word and her afflictions are the main source of her adoration and devotion to Jesus Christ. For her, the focus in all her suffering is not to find answers but to find the Answer, God's Son who suffered for her. Joni would say that Jesus is first and foremost the Son of Man who gave his life so that she might have access to God.

If Brother Lawrence had been able to see far into the future of his fellow journeyman Joni Eareckson Tada, he would have smiled to hear her say, "Without Christ, there is no sense in suffering. Without Christ, there is no presence of God."

An Unconventional Pairing

Brother Lawrence lived through the drudgeries of kitchen duty during the 1600s while Paris roiled in the waters of a turbulent France. In this space, he found the secret to peace: being in constant conversation with the Father . . . every day and every hour . . . practicing the presence of God. Brother Lawrence mostly refers to God the Father in *The Practice of the Presence of God*.

While Joni refers to God in all three of his persons, she most often addresses Jesus in this book. After forty years in Christian publishing, I confess that I've never met anyone who has the kind of constant communication with Jesus Christ that Joni experiences. She sings to Jesus as she rolls down her office corridors; she praises him when welcoming everyone she meets; she cheers the Lord for every visiting group that comes into her ministry building. And she also praises God when times are not good—like when she suffers unrelenting pain. She practices the presence of Jesus daily.

How did Brother Lawrence experience such closeness to Jesus, to God, in the seventeenth century, and how does Joni do the same today in the twenty-first? This book will give you a glimpse into the answer.

The Practice of the Presence of Jesus brings Lawrence's and Joni's words together to teach us how to live 24/7 in the peace of their Shepherd. In an inspirational and worshipful way, Lawrence's sayings and Joni's never-before-published meditations and stories strengthen each other to create something fresh and new. Joni's ink sketches, which she rendered holding a pen between her teeth, are also included. *The Practice of the Presence of Jesus* will help you find a daily rhythm of experiencing the nearness of God in simple yet dramatic ways. Brother Lawrence and Joni trade their thoughts back and forth, making a beautiful song to God. It is the timeless, lilting melody of being with Jesus.

—JOHN SLOAN
Editor Emeritus

Before You Begin

Suffering has a way of heaving you beyond the shallows of life where your faith tends to feel ankle-deep. It casts you out into the fathomless depths of God, a place where Jesus is the only One who can touch bottom.

For more than half a century, at every age, my quadriplegia has taught me how to swim in the depths of God. I am not saying that I swim well. Sometimes I feel like I'm only dog-paddling. Other times I think I'll drown in the waves of pain that crash over me. But Jesus is always my rescuer. He is my anchor, and I cling tighter to him now than ever before. It's because I need him more.

Pain never lets up. It pushes you to limits where you nearly collapse. And sometimes you do. But pain has also melded my heart with my Savior's. I find comfort in the Man of Sorrows who is acquainted with grief (see Isaiah 53:3); he is a better relief and rest than any pain medication.

And it is my pain that has forced a slower pace. I now see

more in his Word. I see Jesus in small and great pleasures. I feel his delight in everything from sun-dappled shadows on a lawn to those breathtaking moments when a wayward soul awakens to gospel truth. Everything means more to me now. Somehow, pain—and perhaps aging—has helped me appreciate life more.

It's why over the last year or so, I've gone back to my tattered copy of *The Practice of the Presence of God*. I remembered how Brother Lawrence's writings first touched me at a younger age when I was healthier and more active. Back in the 1960s, I read Lawrence's little book because everyone was reading it. But now, in a tense post-Covid world, I can say I started reading it again because I knew I would delight in this unassuming monk's approach to life.

Our culture screams at us in a thousand different voices, and at times I can hardly hear my soul breathe. In *The Practice of the Presence of God,* I find the single voice of a humble brother who lowers the volume. His writing is simple, and I like that. Lawrence exercises his faith among pots and pans, scrub buckets, toilets, and dirty floors. . . . I exercise my faith among urine bags, bedpans, wheelchair batteries, support stockings, and an external ventilator.

Life for both the monk and me seems filled with the mundane. But it is also filled with the splendorous majesty of our great triune God.

Lawrence's writing has inspired me. In the ordinary rhythms of life with a disability and its paraphernalia, I practice the moment-by-moment presence of Jesus Christ. I hardly have a choice in the matter; pain and disability require daily close-ness to Christ.

As I have lately journaled what I am seeing and observing about Jesus's presence and about life overall—especially in our dark, frenetic world—I feel my reflections mirror those of Brother Lawrence. But our meditations are not exactly the same. Our seventeenth-century brother references God. I most frequently point to Jesus and his Word.

After pages of journaling, one thing has led to another. And here you are, holding it all in a collection called *The Practice of the Presence of Jesus*. The idea for this volume can be traced to my longtime editor and friend, John Sloan. I'll never forget carefully leafing through his 1896 edition of Brother Lawrence's classic. The pages were yellowed and well-worn from much use. It's obvious my friend John has a great respect for the modest monk, so when he read a few of my devotional entries, he suggested, "Why not put these to-gether with Lawrence's writings?" And the book you have in your hands is the result.

Each entry in this book includes a time-honored vignette from Lawrence followed by related offerings from my own pen. My devotional reflections occasionally reference Law-rence's, but not always. Rather, I just elucidate his key themes. In this small, sturdy book, my intention is to provide scrip-tural handholds that can move you forward in your aware-ness of Christ's presence and in your daily dialogue with him.

If my Carmelite friend were sitting next to me, I think he would invite you to absorb both his words and mine with the same patience and expectancy modeled in our lives. Never rushing. Waiting always. Enduring long. Not scorning the simple tasks of your days. Seeing God in all things. So linger over this book, and give time for each of our reflections to sink in. There is depth and wisdom to be unearthed here.

—JONI EARECKSON TADA
Joni and Friends International Disability Center

The Practice
of the
Presence of
Jesus

1

Wholly Devoted to Him

I know that for the right practice of the presence of God, the heart must be empty of all other things; because GOD will possess the heart *alone;* and as He cannot possess it *alone,* without emptying it of all besides, so neither can He act *there,* and do in it what He pleases, unless it be left vacant to Him.

— Brother Lawrence, page 42

HE covers the heavens with clouds
and prepares rain for the earth. Ps. 147

I love practicing the presence of my Savior in the dark of night when I cannot sleep. Rather than contend with anxiety, I empty out my heart and pour the beauties of Jesus into it. I fill it with love words for him, each borrowed from the Bible: "Oh, Jesus, to me you are altogether lovely, the fairest of ten thousand, the bright and morning star, my Bridegroom for whom I long. You are the Rose of Sharon, the Lily of the Valley. 'Your love is more delightful than wine. . . . Your name is like perfume poured out'" (Song of Songs 1:2–3). The heart cannot stay filled with muddled thoughts when its hollows are overflowing with the loveliness of Christ.

The next morning I feel refreshed for having lingered in Christ through the night. I wake up a slightly changed person—more settled and content. It's a feeling that God is happy with me. But it's not the smug feeling of being more holy or more righteous or sensing that I have impressed God for having focused so much on his Son; rather, I feel *less* holy. I am *more* aware of my sin, less convinced of my stainless reputation. The fact that I feel more like Paul, the chief of sinners, is an indication that my heart is now a set-apart dwelling where the Spirit of Jesus is pleased to reside. My beautiful Savior has revealed my ugliness of soul, and I fall before him, happy that he is what my heart needs. He's my everything, my all in all.

Meditate: What competes in your heart today with your affection for Jesus?

2

My King

My King, full of mercy and goodness, very far from chastising me, embraces me with love, makes me eat at His table, serves me with His own hands, gives me the key of His treasures; He converses and delights Himself with me incessantly, in a thousand and a thousand ways, and treats me in all respects as His favourite. It is thus I consider myself from time to time in His holy presence.

—Brother Lawrence, page 34

Our great King is eager to pour favor on his children. He does not wait for us to come to him; he seeks us out. He is *actively* pursuing us. One Bible version translates Psalm 23:6: "Indeed, goodness and mercy will pursue me all the days of my life" (NABRE). God pursues us with goodness *by giving us things we haven't earned,* such as warm friendships, food on the table, peace and safety in our streets, jobs to do, and encouraging words over cups of coffee. God pursues us with mercy *by not giving us what we have earned,* such as judgment. He is quick to forgive and overflowing with love, all because of Jesus. God never grows weary of pouring out mercy and goodness.

But his grace-filled, generous nature goes further: He is a King who enjoys bearing our burdens. He loves to work "for those who wait for him" (Isaiah 64:4, NLT). He delights in serving us. Not only here on earth but in glory. We think of heaven as a place where we will serve Jesus forever. While that is true, the complete picture is even more breathtaking. In Luke 12:37, Jesus says that "he will dress himself to serve and will have them recline at the table, and he himself will come and wait on them" (BSB). Oh, friend, for all of eternity we will praise a Savior who is full of goodness and mercy, a Savior who delights to serve *us*!

Meditate: What burdens might Jesus want to carry for you today?

3

A Miserable Sinner?

Give Him thanks, if you please, with me, for His great goodness towards me, which I can never sufficiently admire, for the many favours He has done to so miserable a sinner as I am.

— Brother Lawrence, page 29

As a little girl dressed in my frilly Sunday best, I'd fold my hands, bow my head, and join our congregation in reciting from the *Book of Common Prayer:* "We acknowledge and bewail our manifold sins and wickedness, which we from time to time most grievously have committed, by thought, word, and deed, against thy divine Majesty."[4] Think it's strange for a child to pray that way? Perhaps. But even then, I knew my little heart was wicked.

Wicked is a cutting word. We instinctively recoil from it, not willing to admit the evil within us. A person does not merely fudge the truth; he is a liar. He doesn't merely cheat; he's a thief. Without Christ, we are at the core, wicked. There exists a bentness in the human heart. But once we embrace Christ, 1 Corinthians 5:7 tells us to "get rid of the old yeast, so that you may be a new unleavened batch—*as you really are.*" In Christ, we *really are* at the core righteous. Yes, from time to time we will sin, as the prayer book says, but it is not in our nature as blood-bought believers to do so habitually. Continuously. Routinely. We have Holy Spirit–help that enables us to be who we truly are. What glorious hope! Today, slice out the serpent of sin that has coiled itself around your heart. Open your soul to the beauties of the gospel and the loveliness of Jesus who rescues you from your transgressions. Ask his Spirit to reinforce your bentness for good and then follow his every prompting to make your heart a worthy home for Jesus.

Meditate: First Corinthians 5:7 is a powerful declaration of your identity in Christ. Think hard on how this should change the way you live.

4

The Crown

Ever since that time I walk before GOD simply, in faith,
with humility and with love; and I apply myself diligently
to do nothing and think nothing which may displease
Him. I hope that when I have done what I can,
He will do with me what He pleases.

—*Brother Lawrence, page 32*

At his coronation in 1804, Napoleon Bonaparte dressed himself in opulent robes, stood, and held the crown above his own head. Everyone else, including the pope, was a mere spectator as he lowered it onto his brow. Napoleon crowned himself emperor of France, demonstrating that he would not be controlled by any power other than himself.[5]

Pride is like that. It crowns itself, ruling over everything wrong about us. But Jesus triumphs over our selfish kingdoms, lovingly insisting we humble ourselves before him. In this humility, we are invited to follow Christ's own example. Jesus "made himself nothing" before his Father, and I must do the same (Philippians 2:7–9). Humility begins with seeing things as they are: God is great, and I am not. He is pure, and I am not. He is light, and the hollows of my heart are dark. He is wise, and I have miles to go. When I see things like this, I am on my way to humility. But humility will escape me if I make anything other than the Lord Jesus Christ my goal. If anyone's crown matters, it's the thorny, bloody one he wore. Yield control of your kingdom to him, and you will possess what no tyrant can claim: true humility.

Meditate: How in your life is humility
related to surrender to Jesus?

5

Trust God at All Times

When I thought of nothing but to end my days in
these troubles [doubts of my salvation and the presumption
of faith] (which did not at all diminish the trust I had in
GOD, and which served only to increase my faith),
I found myself changed all at once; and my soul, which,
till that time, was in trouble, felt a profound inward peace,
as if she were in her centre and place of rest.

—Brother Lawrence, page 32

When I was first injured, I was filled with so many doubts and fears of the future that I couldn't imagine ever mustering enough trust in God. I figured only holier-than-thou saints on bended knee, with eyes closed and hands clasped, could trust God with something as awful as paralysis. Only plaster of paris saints on lofty pedestals could possibly trust him at all times, right?

Psalm 62:8 paints a different picture. Without a hint of exaggeration, the psalmist tells us to "trust in him at all times, O people; pour out your heart before him; God is a refuge for us" (ESV). We *can* trust God at all times—not only when it's convenient or when it makes sense or when it's easy, but also when it's counterintuitive to everything within us. Yes, it is possible to trust God in *every* situation. How? Well, through *Jesus*. He gives the command to trust him, then he provides you the power and the will to do it. The minute you "pour out your heart before him," he animates and energizes your trust in him. The instant you recognize that "God is a refuge for us," he is right there with you, assuring you that you don't have to go it alone. To trust in the Lord at all times may sound daunting, but it is possible as you pour out your heart before him and make him your refuge.

When you learn to trust God at all times, you won't be Mother Teresa, but you will develop faith that is readily available. Your faith will be easily within reach; you will effortlessly and gently take hold of it. Your faith will be there, ready to believe, trust, yield, and celebrate your trustworthy God.

Meditate: What barriers prevent you
from fully trusting God?

6

The Circle of Protection

While I am so with Him I fear nothing;
but the least turning from Him is insupportable.

— Brother Lawrence, page 44

I remember watching old Western movies and seeing a recurring scene: Some pioneers, having come under attack, would circle their covered wagons. They stationed their big prairie schooners end to end, forming a circle with the most vulnerable members of the group in the center, the place of safety and protection.

When David was fleeing his enemies, he found protection in a rocky cave near Adullam. Scholars believe that's when he penned Psalm 34:7, which says, "The angel of the LORD encamps around those who fear him, and he delivers them."[6] The word *encamps* means a "circling around," and we can imagine David looking up and, through faith, marveling at the Lord circling the wagons on his behalf. God was positioning himself on behalf of David: "He encircled him, he cared for him, he kept him as the apple of his eye" (Deuteronomy 32:10, ESV). God's man was in the center of God's ring of protection and strength.

When danger encroaches, put away your fear. Know you are encircled and encompassed by the Captain of the Lord's Army and his angelic host. No enemy can ever force its way through that circle of protection, for "as the mountains surround Jerusalem, so the LORD surrounds his people both now and forevermore" (Psalm 125:2). In that freedom from fear, *we can truly live.*

Meditate: *If today you feel exposed and vulnerable, run into the circle of God's protection.*

7

Mirror Your Savior

Sometimes I consider myself . . . as a stone before a carver,
whereof He is to make a statue: presenting myself thus
before GOD, I desire Him to make His perfect image in
my soul, and render me entirely like Himself.

— *Brother Lawrence, page 35*

Examine Ephesians 1:4 for a minute: "Even before he made the world, God loved us and chose us in Christ" (NLT). Linger on the first part of that verse. Before God created time and space; before he created the universe and declared, "Let there be light" (Genesis 1:3); before he made the world and moved upon the waters, puckered up mountain ranges, ladled out oceans, and carved out rivers; before he created storehouses for the hail, wind, and snow; before all of this, God knew you and loved you. From time immemorial, he imagined and designed you in his heart, envisioning you as he intended you to be.

Since before the foundation of the world, God's finest effort was always . . . *us*. We are created in his image (not even the most beloved animals can claim that). We are God reflectors, mirroring him at every turn. Remember that before there was a sun or moon, before there was day or night, God delighted to place his glory—his image—on you. And there's more! Ephesians 1:4 points to an even higher calling. We bear something about God that's even more specific—"we bear the image of the heavenly man," Jesus Christ (1 Corinthians 15:49). God chose you in Christ to be like *him*. It doesn't get more glorious than that. Today, practice the presence of Jesus by reflecting him to others. Mirror your Savior inside and out. It's what God intended from the beginning of time.

Meditate: What are new ways you can mirror the beautiful image of God?

8

Cry Aloud

A little lifting up the heart in prayer suffices; a little remembrance of GOD, one act of inward worship, though upon a march, and sword in hand, are prayers, which however short, are nevertheless very acceptable to GOD; and far from lessening a soldier's courage in occasions of danger, they best serve to fortify it. . . .

I recommend that you think of GOD the most you can, in the manner here directed; it is very fit and most necessary for a soldier, who is daily exposed to dangers of life, and often of his salvation.

— Brother Lawrence, pages 37–38

He committed adultery, connived, murdered, and spilled the blood of thousands, yet the Lord said of him, "I have found David son of Jesse, a man after my own heart; he will do everything I want him to do" (Acts 13:22). When God looked into David's heart, he saw a desperate sinner who knew himself. The mighty king of Judah confessed, "I am poor and needy, but the Lord takes thought for me. You are my help and my deliverer; do not delay, O my God!" (Psalm 40:17, ESV).

When our souls are straying, it's no time to be subtle. Be like the psalmist who lifted his voice and pleaded, "My heart and my flesh cry out for the living God" (Psalm 84:2). Cry out, groan aloud, persistently plead, show some emotion, and wail; get down and travail. Attach urgency to your prayer; show God you have concern for your endangered soul.

When we call out to the living God, we connect our emptiness with his reservoir of endless power. It's why I have become thankful for my quadriplegia. When at first it spiraled me down into a drain of despair, I panicked and cried out to God. When I sensed his strong arms lifting me out of the pit, I knew I had found lasting help. And now, my quadriplegia affords me a never-ending neediness for the Lord. Do you recognize your soul's need for God? Or are you too worried about your plight to do anything about it? Be as the king of Judah; be poor, needy, and dependent. Do not care what others think, only cry aloud to God for help.

Meditate: If you sense your soul is in peril today, call out to God.

9

Knowing God

We must *know* before we can *love*. In order to *know* GOD, we must often *think* of Him; and when we come to *love* Him, we shall then *also think* of Him often, *for our heart will be with our treasure.*

—Brother Lawrence, pages 51–52

If I want to love Jesus more—and I do—then I must strive to know him better. And knowing Jesus better always gives rise to obedience, for he says, "If you love me, you will keep my commandments" (John 14:15, ESV). This is not a stern or shaming statement; it's more like a promise. It's like Jesus is saying, "If you love me, if you make me the center of your thoughts, if you delight in me and do your most ordinary tasks with an eye to my glory, if you pursue me, then wild horses will not be able to stop you from obeying me." But there's more. Jesus adds, "Whoever has my commandments and keeps them . . . I will love him and *manifest myself to him*" (John 14:21, ESV). Your obedience prompts Jesus to peel back layer after layer of his heart, showing you the secrets of himself: his beauty, worthiness, and things that'll take your breath away. I never used to cry at sunsets or sit for long moments by a flowerbed, reflecting on God's glory; I never used to burst into worship at the sight of snow-covered mountains—but my eyes are now open to these blessings because I keep his commands (Psalm 119:56). So treasure his commandments, for Jesus wants you to know him and love him more. We are blessed—supremely happy—not when we have everything going for us, but when everything in us is going for God.

Meditate: Your simplest pleasures are gifts
from God. Celebrate that.

10

A Holy Freedom

I do not say that therefore we must put
any violent constraint upon ourselves.
No, we must serve GOD in a holy freedom.

— Brother Lawrence, pages 44–45

I love the happy command in Psalm 100:2: "Serve the LORD with gladness!" (ESV). My friend Kenzie does exactly that. Ask her for help, and she will smile and say, "I'm on it!" She makes asking for help a pleasure. And her glad-hearted willingness to lose herself on behalf of another turns up the wattage on God's glory. When Kenzie is in that zone, she is imitating Jesus Christ who "did not come to be served, but to serve, and to give his life as a ransom for many" (Mark 10:45). Kenzie is giving her life so that through her Christ-emulating love, people's hearts might be stirred and made hungry for her God. In that way, her service becomes part of his redemptive plan. Her life is a witness to his eternal love.

Charles Spurgeon said of God: "He is the Lord of the empire of love, and would have his servants dressed in . . . joy."[7] Today, forget yourself as you get underneath others to lift them up; serve them in a way that makes them hungry for what you have. Let them feel your tenderness even if you must sacrifice. Let your kindness shine despite the pain and inconvenience. You'll be serving as Jesus served, and it will stir people's hearts for his love that emanates through your deeds. Such noble, selfless service will command the attention of the universe and cause your joy to overflow.

Meditate: Someone has a greater need than you do. Find that hurting one and fill their emptiness.

11

All Are Sinners

As for the miseries and sins I heard of daily in the world,
I was so far from wondering at them, that, on the
contrary, I was surprised there were not more, considering
the malice sinners were capable of. For my part,
I prayed for them, but knowing that GOD could remedy
the mischiefs they did, when He pleased,
I gave myself no farther trouble.

— Brother Lawrence, page 9

Never once was Jesus casual about human sin. He always faced such darkness head-on, knowing ultimately that sin would be the death of him. And finally, when the Man of Sorrows collapsed in the Garden of Gethsemane, he groaned, "My soul is overwhelmed with sorrow to the point of death. . . . My Father, if it is possible, may this cup be taken from me" (Matthew 26:38–39).

This cup of suffering was so dreadful it was enough to make Jesus recoil in horror: "Being in agony he prayed more earnestly; and his sweat became like great drops of blood falling down to the ground" (Luke 22:44, ESV). As the Savior was shaken to the core, a foul odor must have wafted— not around Jesus's nose but around his heart. Even then, hours before his crucifixion, human wickedness was beginning to crawl upon his spotless being. In that garden, the Apple of the Father's eye was beginning to turn brown with the rot of our wickedness. Jesus was about to drown in raw, liquid sin as God's stored-up rage against humankind exploded in a single direction—at him on the hill of Calvary.[8]

True, God remedied our "mischief," but, oh, at such a cost! So I practice the presence of Jesus every time I take sin seriously and refuse to sweep small sins under the carpet of my conscience. God forbid that I should ever call an offense against God tiny when it has caused my Savior unimaginable pain. May I never minimize the sin that made him suffer.

Meditate: You will never plumb the depths of what happened on the cross . . . but you can try.

12

Return with Praise

We may continue with Him our commerce of love, persevering in His holy presence, one while by an act of praise, of adoration, or of desire: one while by an act of resignation, or thanksgiving, and in all the manner which our spirit can invent.

— Brother Lawrence, page 45

After I spend a lot of time with Jesus in heaven, there's someone I want to meet. We hear about him when Jesus traveled through Samaria and encountered ten men with leprosy. The sad and sorry group stood at a distance and yelled, "Jesus, Master, have pity on us!" (Luke 17:13). The Lord told them to go to the priests; they went, and they were cleansed. But no one went back to thank Jesus. Well, except one. The tenth leper returned "praising God in a loud voice. He threw himself at Jesus' feet and thanked him" (Luke 17:15–16). That's the guy I want to meet. He was as profuse in his thanks as in his plea for help—he did both. *Loudly.*

Like the tenth leper, I have a disability. Like him, I have called out to Jesus countless times. Yes, even loudly, saying, "Oh, Jesus, have mercy. Help me! I need you, Jesus!" And as many times as I have cried out, Jesus has shown me mercy and given me help. Sometimes it's in the form of a friend; other times, it shows up through courage and perseverance. And like leper number ten, I am always running back to the Lord to thank him. Usually loudly.

The more you thank God, the more thankful you'll be. So spur your heart toward gratitude. Persevere in your appreciation for small touches from God that you would normally overlook. He'll open your eyes to his myriad mercies and bless you with a grateful spirit that is commensurate with his greatness. I imagine that when I meet the tenth leper in heaven, we will grasp each other's shoulders, laughing, crying, and blubbering, "Wasn't Jesus just the *best* to us? So generous and merciful!" Then we will jump up and down like schoolkids, making heaven's rafters ring for all of eternity with our boisterous praise of God.

Meditate: Go outside and make a noisy litany to God of things for which you're thankful.

13

Such an Assurance

If sometimes I am a little too much absent from that *Divine presence,* GOD presently makes Himself to be felt in my soul to recall me; which often happens when I am most engaged in my outward business: I answer with exact fidelity to these inward drawings, either by an elevation of my heart towards GOD, or by a meek and fond regard to Him, or by such words as love forms upon these occasions; as for instance, *My* GOD, *here I am all devoted to Thee:* LORD, *make me according to Thy heart.* And then it seems to me . . . that this GOD of love, satisfied with such few words, reposes again, and rests in the . . . centre of my soul.

—Brother Lawrence, *page 39*

Every day, my life is a cosmic battlefield where the mightiest forces of the universe converge in warfare, so I stay alert to the commands of Christ, "the captain of [my] salvation" (Hebrews 2:10, KJV). I know I am genuinely practicing the presence of Jesus when I suit up "like a good soldier of Christ" and "put on the full armor of God" (2 Timothy 2:3–5; Ephesians 6:10–18).

After all, I'm a threat to the devil. At least I *want* to be! He does not waste his time on those who are lukewarm. He has already captured their hearts, so there's no need to fiercely attack them. Oh, may I *never* be lukewarm! When I'm at my lowest—when I feel dull and lethargic in spirit—I remind myself of wartime realities: God is never absent from my life; he is always *for* me. Jesus constantly intercedes for me in my weakness, preserving my soul. The Holy Spirit never tires when it comes to fighting for me, keeping me, and safeguarding me. All of God's holy angels stand ready.

The stakes in this war are immeasurably high, but they are usually fought on the small, ignorable battlefields of everyday life. It is easy to become distracted and tired, but we must never let the Enemy exploit our lowest moments. All of heaven is leaning over the battlements and cheering us on, so let us summon our courage to meet our enemy in the power of the Captain of our souls.

Meditate: Are you holding the shield of faith today, and is the sword of the Spirit in your hand?

14

Saint and Sinner

Sometimes I considered myself before Him as a
poor criminal at the feet of his judge; at other times
I beheld Him in my heart as my FATHER, as my GOD.

— *Brother Lawrence, page 28*

I often feel the same way Brother Lawrence felt in these
lines. Sometimes I see myself as a sinner unworthy of
God's attention. Other times I see myself as his beloved
child nestled happily in his lap. So which is it? The paradox
of our salvation is that it's *both*. We live in that complexity.
Ephesians 2:8 says you "*have been* saved" (that's the beloved child part), yet 1 Corinthians 1:18 says you "*are being*
saved" (that's the sinner part). You are both saint *and* sinner.
So was Lawrence. So am I. Growing in maturity means remembering that these are both part of our present spiritual
reality.

Be careful not to celebrate the "saint" at the expense of the
"sinner." Do not only see yourself as that little child in the
Lord's lap. Because everything changes after you first say yes
to Christ as your Lord and Savior. No longer is it "God loves
you exactly the way you are"; it's "God loves it when you die
to the sins that killed his Son" (see 1 John 3:6). You will never
get beyond the gospel. What saved you in the past is still saving you now. Strive today to be less the sinner and more the
saint. Don't give yourself wiggle room to judge yourself by
your own standards or think that God is satisfied with the
way you live. Judge yourself by the Word, for God won't be
satisfied until the final Day when you "*shall . . . be* saved"
(Romans 5:9). That's when the gospel will have completed its
glorious work, and you will stand beside your Brother and
Bridegroom, Jesus, as pure and spotless as he.

Meditate: Be the child who sits on the King's lap.
When you see the harsh reality of your sin, run to your Father.
He always welcomes his repentant children.

15

He Is There

But those who have the gale of the HOLY SPIRIT, go forward even in sleep. If the vessel of our soul is still tossed with winds and storms, let us awake the LORD, Who reposes in it, and He will quickly calm the sea.

— Brother Lawrence, page 41

Years ago, I was flying through a fierce storm that violently shook our plane. The flight attendant tried to quiet everyone's nerves, but with each jolt and lightning flash outside, passengers gasped and cried out. All except one. A businessman across the aisle from me sat back with his arms folded and head nodding. He slept like a baby through the whole thing!

I think of him when I read the account of Jesus sleeping through a storm in a boat that was about to capsize (he, too, was exhausted and was probably trying to grab a few winks). As the boat took on water, his disciples became frantic, crying, "Master, carest thou not that we perish?" (Mark 4:38, KJV). They called Jesus their Master, but their cry was tinged with fear to the point of sarcasm. They didn't understand why Jesus wasn't exercising his power to rescue them. I feel the same when pain, like a squall, nearly sinks me. Knowing that Jesus may not immediately bring relief is unnerving. *But wait,* I tell myself, *he's in the boat.* Despite appearances, that fact means I am in the safest place in the world. It is enough that he is in the boat with me. Resting in him, I cannot sink.

Ezekiel 48:35 says, "The LORD IS THERE." You could be sitting in HR facing an unexpected exit interview. He is there. Or waiting at the doctor's office for your MRI results. He is there. Your heart can remain untroubled, for "no water can swallow the ship where lies the Master of ocean and earth and skies."[9] Wherever you are, he is *there.*

Meditate: What cares and worries can
you cast on Jesus today?

16

The Spiritual Life

We must . . . always work at the spiritual life, because
not to advance, in the spiritual life, is to go back.

— Brother Lawrence, page 41

What would you think of an athlete who skips practice before the big game? You probably wouldn't call her diligent. Or the tenth grader who shuts his books after fifteen minutes of study? Is he a diligent student? Not at all. What about someone who says they really want to know Jesus? Hebrews 11:6 says that God "is a rewarder of them that diligently seek him" (KJV). The proof of your desire to know Jesus is your diligence in seeking him.

If we diligently seek him, then we work out our salvation with trembling; we act on our redemption and make it real through our lived-out preferences for Christ. We strive to produce the effects of our salvation, showing proof of our sonship by obedience. Though we have *found* him, with joy we will continue to *seek* him for a lifetime. The good news? The instant you make Jesus your hot pursuit, then divine energy surges through you, fulfilling what God expects from one of his purchased ones. God will then reward your earnest soul effort with a sweet, intimate friendship with his Son. Such a prize is *more* than worth the work.

Meditate: Every day you're either
striving toward Jesus or drifting away.
Which describes you?

17

Kingdom Work

We must do our business faithfully, without trouble or disquiet; recalling our mind to GOD mildly and with tranquility, as often as we find it wandering from Him.

—Brother Lawrence, page 45

I once designed a T-shirt for the women who help me get up in the morning. I printed Colossians 3:23–24 on the back: "Whatever you do, work at it with all your heart, as working for the Lord, not for human masters, since you know that you will receive an inheritance from the Lord as a reward. It is the Lord Christ you are serving." Some might say that giving a bed bath, emptying a urine bucket, wiping mucus, or brushing someone else's teeth are tasks too menial to be considered the Lord's work. But these things *are* kingdom work. Each lowly task is sacred because my helpers are "working for the Lord." In turn, I work for the Lord as I pray for each woman and her needs.

As far as your Savior is concerned, there are no small or insignificant jobs in his realm (which extends to laundry rooms, college dorms, assembly lines, and office cubicles). Nothing you do in the name of Jesus is ever useless or pointless. As Paul wrote, "My dear brothers and sisters, stand firm. Let nothing move you. Always give yourselves fully to the work of the Lord, because you know that your labor in the Lord is not in vain" (1 Corinthians 15:58). When you give yourself fully in service to Jesus, no job is too menial. Each job matters. So practice the presence of Jesus today: Smile and wash your roommate's dirty dishes.

Meditate: Today when you take out trash,
sing a worship song all the way to the curbside.

18

God's Joy

Judge by this what content and satisfaction I enjoy, while
I continually find in myself so great a treasure: I am
no longer in an anxious search after it, but have it open
before me, and may take what I please of it.

—Brother Lawrence, pages 39–40

God is *crazy* about you. You are his treasured possession, the apple of his eye, precious and honored in his sight (Deuteronomy 7:6; Isaiah 43:4; Zechariah 2:8)! God's utter delight in you is described in Zephaniah 3:17, which says, "He will rejoice over you with gladness; . . . He will rejoice over you with singing" (BSB). That word *rejoice* literally means to dance, skip, and leap with joy.

But before you become enamored with yourself and think you've got God wrapped around your little finger, remember that God's joy in you is related to the way he feels about his Son. When God sees you, he sees Jesus. God takes joy in you through the stunning character of Jesus; he delights in the complexity and wonder of all that your Savior has done. God's joy in you is all wrapped up in Christ, for "God has united you with Christ Jesus. For our benefit God made him to be wisdom itself. Christ made us right with God; he made us pure and holy, and he freed us from sin" (1 Corinthians 1:30, NLT).

Never let it escape you that once you "were by nature [a child] of wrath, like the rest of mankind" (Ephesians 2:3, ESV). Ah, but that has now changed, for you are a child of the King. And when you love and obey him, you become a sweet, fragrant offering that reminds God of the sacrifices of his own Son which, in turn, further magnifies God's great joy in you. It's a wondrous circle of love, always spiraling upward in greater glory to Jesus and greater happiness in our hearts!

Meditate: How does your obedience rise like a sweet fragrance to God?

19

A Wholesome Remedy

Dear friend, GOD has given you a good disposition, and a good will; but there is in you still a little of the world, and a great deal of youth. I hope the affliction which GOD has sent you will prove a wholesome remedy to you, and make you enter into yourself; it is an accident very proper to engage you to put all your trust in *Him,* Who accompanies you everywhere: think of Him the oftenest you can, especially in the greatest dangers.

— *Brother Lawrence, page 37*

B rother Lawrence said that his friend possessed "a little of the world, and a great deal of youth." That describes me perfectly as a seventeen-year-old. I claimed Christ as Lord, yet you'd be hard-pressed to believe it, given the way I carried on with my boyfriend on Friday nights. I felt remorse over my sexual sin, and I confessed it every Sunday morning, but after a year of this sad cycle, I knew I was trapped. Lust had enslaved me, and I was unable to break free. Then I read 1 John 2:4: "If anyone says, 'I know [Jesus],' but does not keep His commandments, he is a liar, and the truth is not in him" (BSB). God help me, I did *not* want to live a lie anymore!

So I cried out, "Jesus, *do* something—anything! I'm powerless to turn my life around!" Now, I'm not saying that a broken neck was God's answer to that prayer. Yes, Hebrews 12:6 says that God disciplines those he loves, just as a wise earthly father corrects his beloved children who go astray, but only heaven will reveal the Lord's purpose behind my accident. I *can* say this about Hebrews 12. It is a warning. It is a powerful, yet unsettling, statement about the gracious sovereignty of God in rescuing his people from their choices that lead to death, specifically spiritual death. So before your private disobedience enslaves *you,* let this quadriplegic gently warn you with Proverbs 19:16: "One who keeps the commandment keeps his soul, but one who is careless of conduct will die" (NASB).

Meditate: Afflictions are not always
God's discipline. But whatever his reason,
his discipline is always for your good.

20

To Be *with* God

It is not necessary for being with GOD to be always
at church; we may make an oratory of our heart,
wherein to retire from time to time, to converse with
Him in meekness, humility, and love. Every one is
capable of such familiar conversation with GOD, some
more, some less: He knows what we can do.

—Brother Lawrence, page 47

The agony of my physical afflictions can often wear me down. Sometimes I can barely speak a word of worship, let alone think straight. That's when my praise is reduced to whispering one phrase over and over: "Jesus Christ, Son of God, ruler of heaven and earth." I breathe those ten words in and out, inhaling and exhaling my offering to God. Like Brother Lawrence says, God knows what I can do. And as my little worship rises to heaven, my generous Savior makes far more of it than its skimpy nature deserves.

When my worship seems fragile and feeble, when my heart is muddied with misgivings, Jesus does not impatiently tap his foot, fold his arms, look at his watch, and think, *This girl better get her worship on.* He graciously remembers I am made of nothing but mud. Psalm 103:13–14 assures me that "just as a father has compassion on his children, so the LORD has compassion on those who fear Him. For He Himself knows our form; He is mindful that we are nothing but dust" (NASB). My soul occupies a pain-filled pile of dust, yet when I esteem Christ as worthy, he enlarges my little praise. Even when it's reduced to ten words, he knows my intentions and is aware that I am made of only earth. I am like Mary whose tears quietly mingled with her simple act of perfume-scented worship. Jesus looked on her kindly and said of her, "She did what she could" (Mark 14:8). He graciously does the same for me and you.

Meditate: Do *what you can to fill this day
with grateful thoughts toward* God.

21

Infinite Treasure

I complain much of our blindness; and cry often that we are to be pitied who content ourselves with so little. GOD . . . *has infinite treasure to bestow, and we take up with a little sensible devotion, which passes in a moment. Blind as we are, we hinder God, and stop the current of His graces. But when He finds a soul penetrated with a lively faith, He pours into it His graces and favours plentifully.*

—Brother Lawrence, page 40

Recently, my Sunday night caregiver moved out of town, and I fretted over who would replace her. I put my need to prayer, and in good time, God provided a new helper. Actually, two helpers. Philippians 4:19 assures us that "God will meet all your needs according to the riches of his glory in Christ Jesus." Our greatest need can never exceed the abundant resources that are ours in Christ. He is incomprehensibly rich; he is the vast and only reservoir of help for every want. Only Jesus can fill a need with "a good measure, pressed down, shaken together and running over" (Luke 6:38). It's why our Savior looks so glorious!

The Puritan Thomas Brooks perfectly describes the wellspring of wealth that is ours in Christ:

> There is in a crucified Jesus—something proportionable to all the straits, wants, necessities, and desires of His poor people. He is bread to nourish them, and a garment to cover and adorn them, a physician to heal them. [Jesus is] a counseller to advise them, a captain to defend them, a prince to rule, a prophet to teach, and a priest to make atonement for them; a husband to protect, a father to provide, a brother to relieve. [Jesus is] a foundation to support [His people], a head to guide, a treasure to enrich, a sun to enlighten, and a fountain to cleanse. Now what can any Christian desire more to satisfy him and save him, to make him holy and happy in both worlds?[10]

Meditate: Is there a need that's nagging?
Ask God to fill it in his perfect will and timing.

22

Pain, Defanged

I do not pray that you may be delivered from your pains;
but I pray GOD earnestly, that He would give you strength
and patience to bear them as long as He pleases.

—Brother Lawrence, pages 53–54

People who regularly run marathons learn to live with pain. They defang pain of its terror by familiarizing themselves with its nuances and distinguishing features. They don't try to beat pain; instead, they carry it with them, managing and minimizing it as best they can. I do the same. When pain becomes agonizing, I don't fear it. I breathe deeply and enter into it much like the Hebrews who entered into Nebuchadnezzar's fiery furnace. I expect to meet Jesus in it, just as the three Hebrews met the Son of God in the flames.

Expect to meet Jesus in your pain, and you most certainly will. For he has already entered that awful place ahead of you. He transformed it by his power and presence and came out the other side. He uprooted its dread and left it a place of resurrection and hope. So take a deep breath and step into your agony, anticipating that you'll see Jesus. He will give you courage to deliberately look pain in the face, study its stern features, and enter unafraid. Most of all, be patient. Quietly stand in opposition to your fear. Steady your soul and calmly let pain know that it will not and cannot overwhelm you. Your Savior assures, "When you walk through the fire, you will not be scorched. . . . For I am the LORD your God, the Holy One of Israel, your Savior" (Isaiah 43:2–3, NASB). When you approach pain this way, it lessens the discomfort; in your most hellish place, you can meet the King of heaven.

Meditate: Even hellish pain can be heavenly when you find Jesus in it.

23

Trust the Savior

I am very well pleased with the trust which you have in GOD: I wish that He may increase it in you more and more: we cannot have too much trust in so good and faithful a Friend, Who will never fail us in this world nor in the next.

— Brother Lawrence, page 52

The Bible tells me that Jesus is more wonderful, more delightful, and more pleasurable than I can possibly imagine. Although it's "unimaginable," the Bible still urges me to keep pursuing endless delight in Jesus, for "in Your presence is fullness of joy; in Your right hand there are pleasures forever" (Psalm 16:11, NASB). I get so frustrated and disgusted with myself whenever I ignore Jesus and give in easily to worldly pleasures, silly fantasies, or banal, mind-numbing entertainment. I already know these things don't satisfy my soul (they only deaden it). So I resolve to ratchet up the fight to keep choosing Christ. I get back into the boxing ring with renewed vigor, exerting all my strength to stay satisfied in my Savior. I will not give up so easily when I know there is maximum, full-force joy in the Lord awaiting me!

It is a fight to trust Jesus. I must trust that everything my heart could ever long for is wrapped up in him and that he is far superior to anything the world offers. To *not* believe this is to demonstrate an utter lack of trust in my Savior. Oh, how I long for my trust in him to have the upper hand in my heart! So I cry out, "Whom do I have in heaven but You? And with You, I desire nothing on earth" (Psalm 73:25, NASB). Cause me to believe this, dear Jesus; make me taste how satisfying you, the Bread of Life, truly are. May your Word keep feeding my faith's appetite for you and you alone!

Meditate: Fight the good fight today and land a knockout blow against worldly desires.

24

A Clean Heart

I think it proper to inform you after what manner I
consider myself before GOD, Whom I behold as my *King*.
I consider myself to be the most wretched of men, full of
sores and corruption, and who has committed all sorts
of crimes against his King; touched with sensible
regret I confess to Him all my wickedness, I ask His
forgiveness, I abandon myself in His hands, that
He may do what He pleases with me.

—Brother Lawrence, pages 33–34

Not long ago, my husband, Ken, was trying to find something in the garage, and in his search, he literally tore it apart. He opened boxes, dumped buckets, rummaged through files, and turned bags inside out. The garage was ransacked, but finally, Ken found the treasured item; the search proved fruitful.

I think about Ken's frenzied focus when I read Psalm 139:23–24, which says, "Search me, O God. . . . See if there is any offensive way in me" (NIV84). May we have that same feverish focus in searching out our hidden sins! They can be easily found, for the more we connect our sins to the spikes pounded into the body of our Best Friend, the more urgent our search for them. Jeremiah 17:9 says, "The heart is deceitful above all things and beyond cure. Who can understand it?" Well, the Holy Spirit sure does. Even a redeemed heart is in cahoots with sin. I practice the presence of Jesus when I ask him to shine his search-and-destroy spotlight deep inside me. Together we ransack my heart from one chamber to the next; neither of us wants a web of cloaked sins to choke out my warm-hearted devotion to him. Whenever Jesus exposes a mesh of entangled transgressions, I pray, "Rip it out, Lord. And if you catch me toying with this sin again? Slam me with guilt! Do this for your name's sake." Practice Jesus's presence like this, for there's no mission more fruitful than a clean heart.

Meditate: Go on a search-and-destroy mission against things in your life that disappoint God.

25

Near

You need not cry very loud;
He is nearer to us than we are aware of.

— Brother Lawrence, pages 46–47

D ecades ago I was watching astronauts as they repaired the Hubble Space Telescope. NASA explained it was a matter of life-and-death that the astronauts stay tethered to the space shuttle. If somehow they became detached, there was no way they could "swim" their way back to safety, even if the shuttle were inches within reach. At zero gravity and with no object against which they could push to reach their ship, they'd be stranded in space. The idea terrified me.

The height of terror is to sense that the distance between you and God is unbridgeable. That you are irretrievable and unreachable, a hopeless sinner in the hands of an angry God. That your moral failure has put you on a separate orbital path from him with an entire universe between you. Do not think there's a vast chasm of wrath that separates you from God. Yes, God is great and sovereign, but he is equally filled with goodness, tenderness, gentleness, and compassion. When God revealed himself to Moses, he did not display his wrath against sin; instead, he proclaimed, "The LORD, the LORD, a God merciful and gracious, slow to anger, and abounding in steadfast love and faithfulness, keeping steadfast love for thousands, forgiving iniquity and transgression and sin" (Exodus 34:6–7, ESV).

God is all about rescuing the unreachable and retrieving the irretrievable. The mercy of God reaches across time and space to tether you to himself, your only place of safety. God is *that* good. He is *that* near.

Meditate: Be amazed that God crossed time,
space, and endless galaxies to reach you.

26

Abide in His Promises

All consists in *one hearty renunciation* of everything which we are sensible does not lead to GOD; that we might accustom ourselves to a continual conversation with Him, with freedom and in simplicity. That we need only to recognise God intimately present with us, to address ourselves to Him every moment.

— Brother Lawrence, pages 19–20

In all ways acknowledge Him...
and He will make your paths straight.
Prov. 3

I thrive on the promises of God. They give shape and definition not only to my life in general but also specifically to my days. To practice the presence of Jesus is to wake up every morning and choose a Bible promise to live on for the day. Just one promise. Let's say I wake up feeling weak and in need of strength. I could choose 2 Chronicles 16:9: "For the eyes of the LORD range throughout the earth to strengthen those whose hearts are fully committed to him." Then, throughout the morning, I am aware that God is working to strengthen me. Or if I'm in physical pain, I could choose Psalm 34:19: "The righteous person may have many troubles, but the LORD delivers him from them all." Then, all day long, I rely on God to deliver me from discouragement and defeat. He promises he will!

This is the Christian way to live. A daily promise keeps me from falling into an ambiguous, willy-nilly approach to life. A daily promise becomes a plumb line for my attitudes and actions. Starting every morning with a Bible promise adds such value to my day, helping me make the most of opportunities, build character, and glorify God. So practice the presence of Jesus by abiding in one of his promises: "For no matter how many promises God has made, they are 'Yes' in Christ. And so through him the 'Amen' is spoken by us to the glory of God" (2 Corinthians 1:20). So select a promise, and seize the day!

Meditate: Memorize three promises this week.
They'll be at hand when you need them.

27

Blessed Are Those Who Suffer

Comfort yourself with Him, who holds you fastened to the cross: He will loose you when He thinks fit. Happy those who suffer with Him: accustom yourself to suffer in that manner, and seek from Him the strength to endure as much, and as long as He shall judge to be necessary for you.

—Brother Lawrence, page 54

Real happiness is hard to come by. Many Christians default to the lesser, more accessible joys of our culture. But the more we saturate ourselves with earthy pleasures, the more pickled our minds become, sitting and soaking in worldly wants to the point that we hardly know what our souls need. We then interpret the loan approval, job promotion, and home-team victory as glorious blessings sent from On High. But are they?

Jesus has in mind deeper blessings for us. They aren't so much "physical," like the blessings in the Old Testament—back then, God blessed his people with annihilated enemies, opened wombs, bounteous harvests, abundant rains, and quivers full of children. Jesus takes a different approach. He locates blessings closer to pain and suffering. In his most famous sermon, he lists the following blessings: empty-handed spiritual poverty, a heart heavy with sorrow, a lowly and forgiving spirit, eschewing sin, and experiencing persecution (see Matthew 5:3–10).

How are we to understand these hard-edged things as blessings? I am blessed for the way my suffering has sent me into the inner recesses of God's heart and shut the door on the world. In that solitary get-alone-with-God place, fresh desires for Jesus started springing up in my soul. My love, my devotion, and a sober respect for my majestic Savior began to stretch my capacity for him. I found a lively hope of heaven and a desire to live a holy life. Suffering brought my own emptiness and God's fullness together. And I couldn't imagine any better blessings!

Meditate: Ask God to shift your blessings
focus from the material to the eternal!

28

Goodness in Suffering

I believe it is impossible not only that GOD should deceive, but also that He should long let a soul suffer which is perfectly resigned to Him, and resolved to endure everything for His sake.

— Brother Lawrence, page 17

To echo Brother Lawrence, God will never let a Christian soul suffer harm. You might think, *Wait, I know plenty of believers whose suffering made them bitter; their afflictions did their souls no good.* When pushed up hard against suffering, many Christians will even use Jesus's own words to question God's purposes. These people cannot understand how suffering can be equated with good.

> What person is there among you who, when his son asks for a loaf of bread, will give him a stone? Or if he asks for a fish, he will not give him a snake, will he? So if you, despite being evil, know how to give good gifts to your children, how much more will your Father who is in heaven give good things to those who ask Him!" (Matthew 7:9–11, NASB)

I have lived more than half a century as a quadriplegic and almost as many years in chronic pain, yet never once has God allowed anything that has harmed my soul. Yes, my body is harmed! But *never* my soul. God allows only those things that are designed to strengthen my soul, stretch its capacity for himself, and increase its hunger and thirst for the grace of Jesus.

So for all who question the goodness of God in their suffering, the Spirit of Jesus warns us in Hebrews 12:15 to "be careful . . . that none of you fails to respond to the grace which God gives, for if he does there can very easily spring up in him a bitter spirit which is not only bad in itself but can also poison the lives of many others" (PHILLIPS).

Meditate: In Jeremiah 32:40, God is talking about you when he says, "I will never stop doing good to them."

29

A Taste for Jesus

We ought to love our friends, but without encroaching upon the love of GOD, which must be the principal.

— Brother Lawrence, page 53

Sometimes I see myself as twelve scoops of dark-roasted coffee through which God's grace drips, bringing the rich taste of Jesus into the lives of others. Like the aromatic flavor of a good coffee, I want my life in Jesus Christ to captivate everyone I touch. I want to cultivate in them a taste for Jesus. Whether I pray for, encourage, admonish, or simply bless them, my hope is that others might experience Jesus through me.

Although God remains preeminent in my thoughts and, hopefully, in my motives, I do not view my life in Christ and with others as a hierarchy like God, first; family, second; friends, third; co-workers, fourth; and finally, me, last. My love for Christ and for others is more homogenous than that. More fluid, like coffee. When you make a daily habit of practicing the presence of Jesus, your Christ-infused influence will undoubtedly spill over into the lives of others, for he said, "Whoever believes in Me, as the Scripture has said: 'Streams of living water will flow from within him'" (John 7:38, BSB). Keep yourself close to Jesus, and his life-giving stream will fill your heart, effervesce up into an ecstatic fountain of praise to the Father, and flow out as a steady river of encouragement to everyone around you, bringing refreshment and renewal. To love Christ well is to love everyone well, for there is "one God and Father of all, who is over all and through all and in all" (Ephesians 4:6).

Meditate: How can your words and actions saturate others with Jesus's love today?

30

No Matter What

If we knew how much He loves us, we should
be always ready to receive equally and with
indifference from His hand the sweet and the bitter;
all would please that came from Him.

— *Brother Lawrence, pages 61–62*

After losing his family, his property, his health, his standing in the community, and the respect of his wife, Job makes this astounding statement in Job 2:10: "Shall we accept good from God, and not trouble?" A person only says that if they have a high and healthy respect, as well as fear, of God.

When I first broke my neck, it took a long time before I could agree with Job and accept not only good from God but also the many troubles my wheelchair brought. Things changed when I realized they weren't my wheelchair's troubles. They were God's troubles. That fact alone infused a hefty amount of awe into my view of God. This was the Almighty with whom I was dealing, and even though I still did not understand his ways, I decided I'd rather receive trouble from God's left hand than receive nothing at all. Deuteronomy 29:29 told me, "The secret things belong to the LORD our God, but the things revealed belong to us . . . that we may follow all the words of this law." I may not have understood God's secret things, but I could grasp God's revealed things: Jesus died for me and loves me, and so proved that God can always be trusted with the troubles he sends. If you are perplexed by the secret ways of God in your troubles, always filter them through Jesus, the Way that can be trusted . . . no matter what.

Meditate: In this world we will have trouble . . .
but Jesus can handle it for your sake.

31

The Greatest of Sinners

That we ought, without anxiety, to expect the
pardon of our sins from the Blood of JESUS CHRIST,
only endeavouring to love Him with all our hearts.
That GOD seemed to have granted the greatest
favours to the greatest sinners, as more
signal monuments of His mercy.

— Brother Lawrence, page 15

I see myself trembling, standing blindfolded in front of the firing squad—guilty, condemned, and about to be executed for my sins. Then a kindly man draws me aside, removes my blindfold, and starts to tie it on himself, speaking to me directly, saying, "I love you, and I am taking your place." But before he squares himself to the rifles, he lifts his blindfold, looks me straight in the eyes, and says with great passion, "Now tell others what I've done for you and that my love will do the same for them." Then clasping his hands behind his back, he straightens, faces the squad, and boldly commands, "FIRE!"

That's how I look at what Christ did for me. He not only took my place on the cross (aka the firing squad or gallows or guillotine), but he also took the bullet without flinching and with such exquisite love. It makes me sing, "Amazing love! How can it be? . . . For, O my God, it found out me!"[11] Such love makes me want to change and be a better Joni than I was yesterday. A wiser Joni who falls on her face, humbled at the foot of the cross. More obedient. More devoted to God. I strive to be an uncompromising Joni when it comes to shaking off the sins that placed my Savior in front of his "firing squad." Together, let's be those who love Christ in the way of 1 John 4:19: "We love him, because he first loved us" (KJV). Then let us run to share that good news love with others.

Meditate: Sing your favorite worship song to God in response to today's reflections.

32

The Praise of His Glory

Let us renounce, let us generously renounce,
for the love of Him, all that is not He; He deserves
infinitely more. Let us think of Him perpetually.

— *Brother Lawrence, page 5 1*

Why were you saved? Why was I chosen? For what purpose were we born? These are larger-than-life questions, but their answers are simple. Just read 1 Peter 2:9. Long before the universe was created, God called you out of darkness and into his marvelous light so that you might proclaim the excellencies of Jesus. That same calling is given in Ephesians 1:11–12: "In [Jesus] we were also chosen . . . in order that we . . . might be for the praise of his glory" (NIV84). You were born to make Jesus look great. You were saved to prove to others his trustworthiness. And you were chosen to share this good news with everyone.

Once you start living this way, you will be to the praise of his glory. So start making Jesus look good by how you live. By how you treat your husband, your wife, your children. Make him look good by being honest. By thinking the best of others and not keeping a record of people's wrongs. By subduing rebellious thoughts. And you really make Jesus shine by trusting him, for then you are proving that his Word is utterly reliable. He really is as good as the Bible says he is. And the harder it seems to trust him, the better he looks when you do.

In heaven, it'll all come so naturally. To praise him there will be effortless, for we will finally understand the depth of his grace in covering the worst of our sin. So start practicing for that glorious day. It's our primary occupation on earth; it's why God saved us in the first place.

Meditate: In what ways can you make Jesus look good to others?

33

Trusting Jesus

I expected hereafter some great pain of body or mind . . .
the worst that could happen to me was, to lose that
sense of GOD which I had enjoyed so long.

—*Brother Lawrence, page 18*

When I contracted Covid in 2020, I thought it was a death sentence. But years of dealing with quadriplegia had taught me how to carry even this cross. When I trusted Jesus to see me through and gave it all to him (even if it did mean death), I could feel my Savior take gentle, firm possession of my heart and begin to do a work. Lying in bed with the dangerous virus, struggling to breathe, it was as though the Lord was pressing me, "Joni, do you believe that I will never forsake you? That I am your ever-present help in this trouble? That doubting only makes things worse? Do you believe my grace is sufficient, whether I take you home or assign you to remain? Do you *trust* me?"

I cried, "Lord, where else do I go? You have the words of life!" In the ensuing hours, I felt an odd calmness—almost an indifference to how much it might hurt or how it would all end. Jesus pulled me into his safe shelter so that I could rest in him. And I experienced what G. D. Watson once described:

> When the suffering soul reaches a calm, sweet carelessness, when it can inwardly smile at its own suffering, and does not even ask God to deliver it from the suffering, then it has wrought its blessed ministry . . . then the [cross you carry] begins to weave itself into a crown.[12]

When we give our suffering over to Jesus and sink down into his hard will, he makes every pain work its perfect purpose in our lives.

Meditate: Look back on the painful crosses you've carried. In what ways are they now crowns?

34

Praying the Word of God

I do not advise you to use multiplicity of words in prayer;
many words and long discourses being often the occasions
of wandering: hold yourself in prayer before GOD, like a
dumb or paralytic beggar at a rich man's gate.

—*Brother Lawrence, pages 48–49*

The Pharisees liked to employ God's Word in their prayers, but for all the wrong reasons. They were hypocrites who enjoyed showing off how much they knew. They prayed to impress God and other people. But this doesn't mean *we* shouldn't use God's Word in our prayers . . .

The Bible underscores two things that God honors above all else: his name and his Word. So if we pray "in the name of Jesus," shouldn't we also pray "in the Word"? It's why I like to salt-and-pepper my praise and intercession with phrases from the Bible. God's Word is alive and active, so to "pray the Word" gives a dynamic liveliness to your worship and intercession.

" 'Is not my word like fire,' declares the LORD, 'and like a hammer that breaks a rock in pieces?' " (Jeremiah 23:29). The Bible is the hammer you can use to break down spiritual strongholds. It's the flamethrower that burns away the arguments of the Enemy. First Thessalonians 2:13 speaks of "the word of God . . . which is indeed at work in you who believe." If his Word works in our lives, how much more will it work in our prayers for the kingdom? So pray Psalm 62:8 over a friend who is filled with doubts. Pray James 1:3 if patience is needed. This sort of praying cultivates courage, engages your heart, and enlarges your faith. Do this and give your prayers a divine familiarity that earmarks you as a servant of God who knows how to rightly use the most powerful prayer book ever written: the Bible.

> Meditate: Today be intentional about using
> snippets of Scripture in your prayers.

35

The Practice of the Presence

Were I a preacher, I should above all other
things preach the practice of *the presence of* GOD;
and, were I a director, I should advise all the world
to it: so necessary do I think it, and so easy too.

— Brother Lawrence, page 43

Bless the Lord O my soul,
and all that is within me
bless His holy name.
Psalm 103

God created us for his glory, so when we live for his glory, we are doing the very thing he designed us to do. And, oh, the joy! I live with paralysis and pain, but I feel such pleasure when I trust God through hard times—I'm happily doing what he designed me to do, and it gives him glory. I cannot peel an orange or go for a brisk walk, but I find indescribable delight in a million other blessings he provides. Or when I triumph over temptation, I feel such delight in my obedience. It's because God created me to obey him, and I'm happy following through on his design. Finally, when I introduce someone to Jesus and his gospel, I take enormous pleasure in doing perhaps the most fundamental thing God created me to do: share his good news with a lost world.

My heart is glad when I am living for God's glory (it's the way he intends it). I am most myself; that is, I am who Joni is supposed to be when I gasp in wonder at one of his sunsets or waterfalls or mountain ranges. I am fulfilling my created purpose for living; I am glorifying God by joyously shining the spotlight on his creative genius. Practice Jesus's presence this way every day, making 1 Corinthians 10:31 your guide, for "whether you eat or drink or whatever you do, do it all for the glory of God." This is the secret of practicing the presence of Jesus.

Meditate: In *what ways will you live for the glory of God today?*

36

Run to Jesus

Ah! knew we but the want we have of the grace and assistance of GOD, we should never lose sight of Him, no, not for a moment.

— *Brother Lawrence, page 43*

Sometimes I feel like crying, "Oh, Jesus, save me. The world, the flesh, and the devil are after me, looking to eat my soul alive." Now, you may think, *What a ridiculous overstatement. Lighten up, Joni, and cut yourself some slack.* I don't buy it. I have seen where a click and a scroll will take me, where a song on an old playlist will lead me, or how a little one-upmanship will ruin me. I have witnessed my soul at its worst, comparing and competing and stuffing itself with the dull offerings of this world. Jesus paid too great a price for me to squander my blood-bought soul on the very things that cut him to pieces on his cross. So I stick to 1 Peter 4:1–2:

> Therefore, since Christ suffered in His body, arm yourselves with the same resolve, because anyone who has suffered in his body is done with sin. Consequently, he does not live out his remaining time on earth for human passions, but for the will of God. (BSB)

When I run to Jesus in *my* weakness, I am appealing to *God's* strength. And God responds in an instant, enfolding me in his protective arms. Once I'm there, the world, the flesh, and the devil with all his lesser demons dare not touch me. When I reckon myself "in Christ," the shrill voice of my appetites, the hollowness of self-importance, and all the hounds of the Adversary cannot harm me. It's no overstatement: The world, the flesh, and the devil are hell-bent after you, so arm yourself with the same resolve. Let us live, today and tomorrow, for the will of God.

Meditate: Do not fear the world, the flesh, and the devil. Jesus is bigger than them all.

37

Make Every Effort

Hope in Him more than ever: thank Him with me
for the favours He does for you, particularly for the fortitude
and patience which He gives you in your afflictions:
it is a plain mark of the care He takes of you; comfort
yourself then with Him, and give thanks for all.

— Brother Lawrence, page 36

It is easy to assume the Christian life will automatically happen to us, as if we were in a pinball machine, bouncing off circumstances and thinking that eventually we'll score (and finally get this Christian thing right). Life in Christ is not like that. Second Peter 1:5–6 insists that believers "make every effort to add to your faith goodness; and to goodness, knowledge; and to knowledge, self-control; and to self-control, perseverance; and to perseverance, godliness."

I learned to "make every effort" when I lived on our Maryland farm. I would sit in my wheelchair by the bay window that overlooked the pasture, wishing I could head to the barn, saddle up, and go horseback riding. But I dared not allow my thoughts to wander into a pointless daydream, so I'd pray something like: "Jesus, deep down I know that self-pity is wrong, and I want to do what's right. So I'm putting on spurs and goading my emotions out of their shadowy stall, into the light of day, and up the trail to gratitude. My feelings don't want to go there; they'd rather stay in the barn. But like a rider with a bit and a whip, I'm riding my stubborn feelings hard in the right direction. And as I do, please, Jesus, reward me with a grateful heart. Help me to not only do but feel the right thing!"

Meditate: If today you feel a little lost spiritually,
follow the trail of 2 Peter 1:5–6.

38

A Christian's Profession

Do not then forget Him, but think on Him often, adore Him continually, live and die with Him; this is the glorious employment of a Christian; in a word, this is our profession, if we do not know it we must learn it.

— *Brother Lawrence, page 53*

Understandably, God's people do not want to settle for mediocrity, so we are always looking for a worthy, noble endeavor to which we can give ourselves. Something that will actualize our high calling as followers of Christ; perhaps a platform where our spiritual giftings can shine and bring God the highest glory. God's people are spending an inordinate amount of energy and time searching for something beyond what they already have.

We may not realize it, but we most likely already possess that platform, that sphere of influence, or that exemplary ministry. Almighty God has already called us to be part of the most powerful work of transformation in the history of the universe. It is the same global work for which Christ lived and died (it's *that* important). There is nothing we could possibly strive for that is more worthy or God-honoring. What is this heaven-shaking work? God asks us to partner with him in a highly personal redemptive plan—he wants us to tell our neighbors, family, co-workers, classmates, and friends about salvation in Jesus Christ. It's a calling that involves cosmic concerns like life and death. There is no higher or more noble work than to spread the good news of Jesus. And we begin doing this work by simply and faithfully *living*.

It's your purpose and mine. Don't sit around and wait for something more exciting to happen.

Meditate: Who in your sphere of influence needs to know Jesus? Help them find eternal safety.

39

A Cup of Affliction

The men of the world do not comprehend these truths about suffering, nor is it to be wondered at, since they suffer like what they are, and not like Christians: they consider sickness as a pain to nature, and not as a favour from GOD; and seeing it only in that light, they find nothing in it but grief and distress. But those who consider sickness as coming from the hand of GOD, as the effects of His mercy, and the means which He employs for their salvation, commonly find in it great sweetness and sensible consolation.

— Brother Lawrence, page 54

L ike Jesus in the Garden of Gethsemane, I have asked the Father to remove my cup of suffering. But unlike Jesus, who asked only three times, I have pleaded *countless* times. Slowly, over the years, I timidly began drinking my cup of affliction. When it seemed I had drunk it to the dregs, I finally realized that embracing God's hard will with a grateful spirit is the highest expression of faith in him and the most glorious experience a Christian can have.

When our Savior willingly drank that horrific cup, he demonstrated supreme obedience to his Father. Jesus's flint-like faith proved how much he gladly prized God over his own will. The same can be true for us. To drink the cup God has assigned you opens the way to the most glorious of all delights in the Christian life and shows that you treasure God's will above your own. It also demonstrates the depth of your love for God as you squelch all complaints and drink your hard circumstances to the dregs. It is clear to all—especially to the watching world—that you rank him far above what suffering has cost you. You are following in the footsteps of Jesus who walked out of Gethsemane, picked up his cross, and stumbled his way up the bloody hill of Calvary. God the Father glorified Jesus for his obedience, and God will magnify that same Jesus in your life. Does it lessen the weight of your cross? Maybe not. But its weight is heavy enough to ensure that you will keep leaning on him.

Meditate: One day the pain of your cross will be exchanged for the pleasure of a crown.

40

Hope Deferred

Knock, persevere in knocking, and I answer for it that
He will open to you in His due time, and grant you
all at once what He has deferred during many years. . . .
Pray to Him for me, as I pray to Him for you.

—Brother Lawrence, page 61

The words from Proverbs 13:12 describe life as it is: "Hope deferred makes the heart sick, but a longing fulfilled is a tree of life." How many times have you had your hopes raised only to see them dashed? One minute you are flying high; the next, everything's ambushed. That's how I felt shortly after the accident that paralyzed me. At first, I had hopes that I might recover, so I prayed for miraculous healing. But after hundreds of prayers, being anointed with oil, confessing sin, and going to scores of healing services, it was clear I would never walk away from my wheelchair. My hopes were crushed; I was heartbroken.

But the proverb does not say that hope *denied* makes the heart sick; it says hope *deferred*. God is not about to deny my good and godly hope of walking again; he has only postponed it. One day, my hopes *will* find fulfillment. In the meantime, God has a far more glorious plan than giving me legs that walk. As a blood-bought disciple of Jesus, I have confidence that his will for me is "good and acceptable and perfect" (Romans 12:2, ESV). God knows that my wheelchair, for now, is the optimal situation for my supreme happiness in Jesus Christ. And I heartily agree. My ultimate healing may be deferred for a time, but I am happy to wait for God's impeccable timing. I'm not only glad to wait, I'm thankful. Having the chance to know Jesus better through my suffering is worth the wait.

Meditate: Jesus promises that healing will happen. . . .
It's just a matter of time.

41

Sin's Deceit

When an occasion of practising some virtue offered,
I addressed myself to GOD, saying, LORD, *I cannot do this
unless Thou enablest me:* and that then I received strength
more than sufficient. That when I had failed in my duty,
I only confessed my fault, saying to GOD, *I shall never do
otherwise, if You leave me to myself; 'tis You must hinder
my falling, and mend what is amiss.* That after this,
I gave myself no further uneasiness about it.

—Brother Lawrence, page 12

There can be no half measures when it comes to ridding myself of garbagy thoughts, sour attitudes, or manipulative ploys. Sin is too clever to be treated half-heartedly. It'll lie, insisting that it's not out to rip my soul to shreds. It'll promise to behave if I would but allow it to tuck itself away in some quiet corner of my heart. But sin never behaves; it always gets worse.

I don't listen to sin's deceit, and you shouldn't either. Listen to God in Colossians 3:8 who tells us to "rid [ourselves] of all such things as these: anger, rage, malice, slander, and filthy language from [our] lips." Let's rid ourselves of all such things. *All* is a far-reaching word. That same all-inclusive word is used when we are told to love the Lord our God with all our heart, soul, mind, and strength; and our neighbor as ourselves (see Mark 12:30–31). When it comes to loving God and others, there can be no half measures.

I used to think I could straddle the fence between the dominion of darkness and the kingdom of light as long as I kept my balance and didn't tumble into the devil's territory. Yet there is no room for straddling; the top of the fence *is* the devil's territory. I cannot be half-holy. God calls me to serve him with my whole heart, all of the time. Yes, I will fail, but Christ's blood covers even that. And by trusting him to stand in my place before a holy God, his death is accepted for mine, and his perfect life is credited to me.

Meditate: Are you straddling the fence spiritually?
Choose Jesus's side.

42

In Little Things

I have always been governed by love, without selfish views; and that having resolved to make the love of GOD the *end* of all my actions, I had found reasons to be well satisfied with my method. That I was pleased when I could take up a straw from the ground for the love of GOD, seeking Him only, and nothing else, not even His gifts.

—*Brother Lawrence, page* 10

The hill across from our house is lined with white pines whose high branches move in winds I cannot even feel at ground level. I look up and delight in the way the upper breezes pull and push the treetops in a rhythmic dance. It never fails to stir my soul, making me wonder if there were trees surrounding Jesus and Nicodemus that night they met. A soft breeze must've stirred, prompting Jesus to say, "The wind blows wherever it pleases. You hear its sound, but you cannot tell where it comes from or where it is going. So it is with everyone born of the Spirit" (John 3:8).

I love capturing moments like these as reasons to relish in the love of Jesus. I look for the streams of his constant affection that are always flooding my way. I can feel his strength moving in on me when my soul is weak. In my heart, I can kneel quietly and expectantly before God's throne, knowing that heaven has yet to pour out its best gifts on me. I love to open my ears to the sounds of his presence, whether in the rustle of leaves or in the sweet tiny bird notes at dawn. It's the way Jesus wants us to move through our days, for "God intended that they would seek Him and . . . reach out for Him and find Him. . . . 'For in Him we live and move and have our being'" (Acts 17:27–28, BSB).

Meditate: Seek Jesus in little things and you will
never fail to find a blessing from his hand.

43

A Little Strength

The goodness of GOD assured me He would not
forsake me utterly, and that He would give me strength
to bear whatever evil He permitted to happen to me;
and therefore that I feared nothing, and had no
occasion to consult with anybody about my state.

—Brother Lawrence, page 18

Often my strength shrivels when pain keeps jabbing and biting. It drains me of my ability to smile, and all my perseverance seems to dry up. I feel limp and empty. But I've been frequently bolstered by Revelation 3:8 where Jesus says to the church in Philadelphia, "I know your deeds. See, I have placed before you an open door that no one can shut. I know that you have little strength, yet you have kept my word and have not denied my name."

Oh, what courage! Jesus says, "Joni, I know your deeds; I see how you have long persevered. I know how long you've lived with pain. In all your struggles, you have not denied my name but have kept my word. So I have placed before you an open door. You do not need to knock; because you only have a little strength, I have thrown it wide open for you. Just know that the less strength you have, the more help and compassion you will find in me. So now, let me pick you up and carry you through the door."

Christ's words to those saints of old are fitting for you. Jesus sees your perseverance and how you have not denied his name. You do not need to push against the door; he has already opened it, for he understands your weakness. He says, "You have little strength, yet." That word *yet* tells you that God has more than enough power to fill you today.

Meditate: Jesus sees you, he knows your need, and he can pour his power on you.

44

Draw Near to God

Pray remember what I have recommended to you, which is, to think often on GOD, by day, by night, in your business, and even in your diversions. He is always near you and with you; leave Him not alone. You would think it rude to leave a friend alone, who came to visit you: why then must GOD be neglected?

— *Brother Lawrence, page 53*

T he power stick on my wheelchair has two speeds: a turtle image for "slow" and a rabbit image for "fast." I usually wheel on rabbit speed, but that doesn't mean I'm not at rest. I am constantly sitting down, immobile, and "still," so I carry with me an enforced serenity. I thank the Lord that my paralysis provides a built-in sense of rest, even when I am on the go.

As I am wheeling here and there, God's presence goes with me, another blessing that comes with my neediness. There should be a bumper sticker on my wheelchair: "My Presence will go with you, and I will give you rest" (Exodus 33:14). No matter where my wheelchair takes me—whether I am busy with the work of the day or struggling to sleep at night—I am constantly aware of the presence of God. Again, I have my paralysis to thank for that, for "before I was afflicted I went astray" (Psalm 119:67). But now? I stay near Jesus. I stay near his Word. How else could I possibly smile in my afflictions?

Today, if you are moving at the speed of life, learn to see your afflictions as an ally. Let your hardships herd you back to Jesus. Affliction does its best work when it constrains you to stay close to him. The Spirit of Jesus is omnipresent, but he is particularly near in your afflictions.

Meditate: "Draw near to God, and he will draw near to you" (James 4:8, ESV).

45

Infinite Love

He is the FATHER of the afflicted, always ready
to help us. He loves us infinitely more than we
imagine: love Him then, and seek not consolation
elsewhere: I hope you will soon receive it.

—*Brother Lawrence, page 59*

We live on this side of eternity "until the day dawns and the morning star rises in your hearts" (2 Peter 1:19). I often wonder what that will be like. Perhaps our faces will grow hot, as our hearts, pounding with resurrection heat, change in a flash, leaving us magnificently glorified. In that same instant, we will finally grasp the depth of God's love. We will see that the whole plan of redemption was the Father's way of securing for his Son the greatest of gifts: us, his bride and joy. With the Daystar rising in our hearts, Christ's kingdom is completed. His matchless name, vindicated. Sin, death, the devil, and his hoards—all of it—judged and destroyed; earth and heaven, restored; the glory of Jesus filling the universe as he is crowned King of kings.

Envision great multitudes of redeemed people in a deluge of radiance. Surrounded by the angelic host, we shall press in line with the great procession of the saved streaming through gates of pearl. We shall join this infinite cavalcade from earth's widest bounds and oceans' farthest coasts, all in one joyous parade. With countless generations, we will lift our diadems before God. "Hallelujah!" we will shout, "For our Lord God Almighty reigns. Let us rejoice and be glad and give him glory! For the wedding of the Lamb has come, and his bride has made herself ready" (Revelation 19:6–7).

So cry with me, "Come, Lord Jesus!" For we will spend all of eternity praising him for his boundless love that rescued us and brought us safely home (see Ephesians 1:6).

Meditate: Hold on a little longer. . . .
Jesus is on his way back!

46

To Be Holy

One does not become holy all at once. . . .
We ought to help one another by our advice,
and yet more by our good examples.

—Brother Lawrence, page 50

I played the piano for many years before my accident, so I am familiar with tuning forks. Without them, there is no possibility of beautiful music. Everything sounds out of whack. "Be holy, for I am holy" is like a tuning fork (1 Peter 1:16, ESV). This verse is like the Holy Spirit striking his tuning fork and resting it gently on your heart. Does God's ancient command resonate with you? Or is there dissonance, revealing your life is off pitch? God wants you to be holy for your own good—your highest good. For when you sanctify yourself and live rightly, then you have made room in your soul "to comprehend . . . the breadth and length and height and depth, and to know the love of Christ that surpasses knowledge, that you may be filled with all the fullness of God" (Ephesians 3:18–19, ESV).

To be holy is simply to seek first the kingdom of God and his righteousness (see Matthew 6:33). To be holy is to want to be like Jesus, for "whoever says he abides in him ought to walk in the same way in which he walked" (1 John 2:6, ESV). "Be holy, for I am holy" is a happy command. So be different from the world. Hunger and thirst after righteousness. Don't try to make your sin respectable, let alone acceptable. If you are to feel at home in heaven—a holy place for holy people—then become familiar with right living here. I daresay if some who claim Christ went to heaven now, they might not like the place.

Meditate: In what ways can you set yourself apart to God?

47

Pleasing God

Let us . . . think often that our only business
in this life is to please GOD, that perhaps all
besides is but folly and vanity.

—Brother Lawrence, page 50

Every Christian longs to please God, and I have found a glorious way to do so: I strive to be the best gift that God can give himself. Each person of the Trinity showers love on the others, and you and I get to be gifts that delight the Father, the Son, and the Holy Spirit. Our church elder John Ford explained it this way:

- Through our adoption, we are a gift—an adopted child—that Jesus and the Spirit present to the Father (see Ephesians 1:5).

- Through our redemption, we are a gift—a bride—that the Father and the Spirit present to the Son (see Revelation 19:7).

- Through indwelling, we are a gift—a temple—that the Father and the Son present to the Spirit (see 1 Corinthians 6:19).[13]

I have the joy of pleasing all three persons of the great triune God, so I strive to be an obedient child so that my Father can take pleasure in me. I prepare myself to be the pure bride so that my Savior will be delighted in me. And I work to be the clean, sanctified temple so that the Spirit will be happy dwelling in me. Do the same, and you can take great joy in fulfilling the purpose for which you were created!

Meditate: Today, delight the Trinity;
be obedient, be pure, and be sanctified.

48

Listen to Jesus

GOD has many ways of drawing us to Himself.
He sometimes hides Himself from us: but *faith*
alone, which will not fail us in time of need, ought
to be our support, and the foundation of
our confidence, which must be all in GOD.

—*Brother Lawrence, page 57*

God is relentless when it comes to getting your attention. Every day, every hour, God is flooding your senses with the knowledge of Christ. God's great desire is that you know his Son and know him well (see Ephesians 1:17). Everywhere in nature, his messages concerning Jesus are visible, ready to awaken your heart and fill your vision. God is tapping you on the shoulder, whispering in your ear, and pointing to Jesus, saying, "This is my Son, whom I have chosen; listen to him" (Luke 9:35). This isn't just anyone speaking; this is God Almighty, the Creator of heaven and earth, the Ancient of Days, the One who sits enthroned in the heavens, talking to *you*. God has been trying to get your attention for a long, long time. All so that you will listen to Jesus.

Marvel at a stunning sunrise, but be aware: it's God communicating, "My Son did this for you." Stand at the edge of a roaring ocean, and hear God telling you, "This majestic power is but a glimmer of what my Son can do in your life." Hike up a mountain, let your backpack slip off, sit, and be stunned by the vastness beneath you; that wide-opened vista is God's handiwork conveying, "This awesome beauty is only a hint of the loveliness you'll find in my Son." God created the world as a signpost pointing to Jesus. Don't miss it. Go to the Word of God, the Bible, which is his final say on things; open it and *listen to him.*

Meditate: What is God saying
to you in this moment?

49

Talk to Your Heart

At the first, one often thinks practicing the presence as lost time; but you must go on, and resolve to persevere in it to death, notwithstanding all the difficulties that may occur.

—Brother Lawrence, pages 45–46

For my heart's sake, I sing, "Prone to wander, Lord, I feel it, prone to leave the God I love; here's my heart; O take and seal it; seal it for thy courts above!"[14] The lyrics perfectly describe the default mode of my heart. Kick it out of gear and into neutral, and it will invariably drift away from the Lord.

"Therefore we must pay much closer attention to what we have heard, lest we drift away from it" (Hebrews 2:1, ESV). Make your heart pay attention to the truth it has heard. Keep it in drive, not drifting. Keep moving forward, striving toward the upward call. Bend your heart toward God. It is extremely clever, so be aware of its deceptions. Keep its nose in Scripture, and when it whines, "I'm bored," talk to your heart and say, "Stick with it!" Hold its feet to the fire and insist on maintaining mastery over it. Do not accept your heart's laziness, and do everything you can to bring it into alignment when God says, "This is the way; walk ye in it!" Do this and your heart will grow to respect your discipline; better yet, it'll grow to love God. For the purer your heart is, the more delighted it will be with Jesus (see Matthew 5:8).

Sound like a fight? Yes, but it is the good fight of Colossians 3:1: "Since, then, you have been raised with Christ, set your hearts on things above, where Christ is."

Meditate: Set your heart on Christ.
He's already set his heart on you.

50

Speaking of Jesus

In order to form a habit of conversing with GOD
continually, and referring all we do to Him;
we must at first apply to Him with some diligence:
but that after a little care we should find His love
inwardly excite us to it without any difficulty.

— Brother Lawrence, page 11

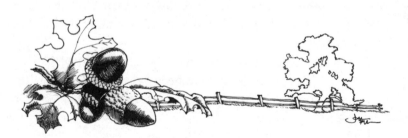

When I am hanging out with Christians, I get a little restless, a tad itchy, when no one brings up Jesus. Then, just when I'm about to offer up words about his gracious goodness to us all, someone will invariably beat me to it—oh, how my heart leaps with joy! All it takes is one person to turn the page in the discussion, and I can almost hear a collective sigh of relief. I glance around, and people's smiles tell me that, together, we have reached home base.

I'm not the only one who responds with joy; listen to Malachi 3:16:

> Then those who feared the LORD talked with each other, and the LORD listened and heard. A scroll of remembrance was written in his presence concerning those who feared the LORD and honored his name.

Think of it. When you and your friends talk fondly together about Jesus, he leans in, listens, and hears what you have to say. That's not all. He then writes down all your good words on a scroll. When you honor the name of the Lord, it is recorded in the presence of the God of the universe. I love to imagine filling the heart of my Jesus with joy, just by speaking glowingly about him with my friends.

If we could only plumb the depths of what Christ sacrificed to secure our salvation, we would talk about him constantly. To everyone, everywhere. Conversing about Christ would not seem out of the ordinary or reserved only for "spiritual interludes"; it would, in fact, seem odd if we failed to speak of him.

Meditate: Before the day ends,
insert Jesus into a conversation.

51

Bring Him Your Pain

While I was troubled in my mind, I had consulted nobody, but knowing only by the light of faith that GOD was present, I contented myself with directing all my actions to Him, i.e., doing them with a desire to please Him, let what would come of it.

—*Brother Lawrence, page 14*

When I am in deep pain, it can make me hunker down, put my shoulder to the grindstone, and mindlessly plow ahead. I tell myself that there's really no need to bring this old, tiresome issue to God, for I know what's causing the agony, anyway: My scoliosis is worsening or my lower vertebrae are pinching. I've been here a thousand times, so why bother God? Or I tell myself shamefully, "I'm in too much pain to pray."

But Jesus *wants* to be bothered. It *pleases* him when we bring him our shame. Pain may insist that prayer will not "make it go away," but prayer always engages me with the power and presence of Jesus Christ, who gladly pours out a deluge of courage, a reservoir of perseverance, a wellspring of endurance and patience, and a marvelous peace that goes far beyond my understanding. When I remember this, it brings Jesus pleasure. He smiles when I listen to his voice rather than the voice of my agonies. It is his joy to elevate me high above the terrain of any dark discomfort when I respond to his whisper, "I have told you these things so that in Me you may have peace. In the world you will have tribulation. But take courage; I have overcome the world!" (John 16:33, BSB). A thousand times, yes. His peace and courage are just as much if not more a miracle than an actual release of my physical affliction. So I will not listen to my pain; instead, "I call on the LORD in my distress, and he answers me" (Psalm 120:1). It is Jesus's pleasure to be my answer.

Meditate: Nothing in your life is too small or insignificant to lay at the feet of Jesus.

52

Seek Him

That we ought, once for all, heartily to put our whole trust in GOD, and make a total surrender of ourselves to Him, secure that He would not deceive us.

—Brother Lawrence, pages 21–22

Have you ever examined a world map and wondered, *How did I land in my country and in my city?* Or looked at your parents and asked, "Why was I born into this family and not another?" I love reading about history, and I often shake my head, wondering, *How come I was born in this century and not the 1700s?* My life would be nothing like it is now! If you were raised across town, or went to a different college, or worked elsewhere, you wouldn't be *you;* the people and circumstances who shape your destiny would be vastly different.

Long before time and space, God planned for you to be exactly where you are and with the specific people you know. But why? The answer is in Acts 17:26–27:

> From one man he made every nation of men . . . and he determined the times set for them and the exact places where they should live. God did this so that men would seek him and perhaps reach out for him and find him, though he is not far from each one of us. (NIV84)

There's no mistaking: God placed you in this century, in this country, in your family, and with your friends for a specific purpose. He arranged the optimal circumstances and put you with the ideal individuals to cause you to seek Jesus, reach out for him, and find him. So don't squander your situation; seek him, for he is not far from you. And be encouraged, for Jesus says, "You will seek me and find me when you seek me with all your heart" (Jeremiah 29:13).

Meditate: How do your circumstances and the people around you make you reach out to Jesus?

53

Preserved in Tranquility

One way to recollect the mind easily in the time of prayer, and preserve it more in tranquility, is not to let it wander too far at other times: you should keep it strictly in the presence of GOD; and being accustomed to think of Him often, you will find it easy to keep your mind calm in the time of prayer, or at least to recall it from its wanderings.

— Brother Lawrence, page 49

If my poor soul had not suffered the bruising and battering of a harsh disability, I would not know half the measure of God's sustaining grace. If my pain had not robbed me of sleep, how could I empathize with the One who had nowhere to even lay his head? Had my wheelchair not confined me, separating me from normal pleasures, how could I know the boundless freedom and joy in Christ, my highest treasure? That my disability, with all its attending troubles, could help others see the glories of Jesus in me?! How did I get *that* honor?

I bear up under an unyielding chronic condition that is always deteriorating, always getting worse with age. But I shoulder every new discouragement, knowing that each pain stretches my soul's capacity for more grace. More of Jesus. More empathy for others. Spurgeon wrote, "There is a lighthouse out at sea: it is a calm night—I cannot tell whether the edifice is firm; the tempest must rage about it, and then I shall know whether it will stand."[15] If all is calm in your life, there is no opportunity for your faith to be strengthened, your hope to glow brighter, or your love to swell with devotion to God and affection for others.

So be the one who welcomes the trial as a friend, endures the hardship as a good soldier, and trusts without badgering God constantly with questions. Then you will kneel in prayer and be at peace, as in a sea of calmness when all around and above the storm rages.

Meditate: In what ways are you growing
through your pain and trials?

54

Hope Overflowing

Let us put all our trust in Him: I doubt not but we shall soon find the effects of it, in receiving the abundance of His grace, with which we can do all things, and without which we can do nothing but sin.

— Brother Lawrence, page 51

When a broken neck upended my life, I didn't know where to turn. God seemed far away, and everything I read in the Bible sounded like a platitude. Then I stumbled upon Isaiah 50:10, "If you are walking in darkness, without a ray of light, trust in the LORD and rely on your God" (NLT). It described me perfectly: in the dark with not a single ray of light. That verse gave me no joy, but it gave *hope*. Something was stirring; it was the faint, magnetic pull toward hope. Honestly, it felt so good to have the fluttering of hope in my heart that I had to act on it. Compelled, I followed this hopeful trail, which led to Romans 15:13: "May the God of hope fill you with all joy and peace as you trust in him, so that you may overflow with hope." I thought, *Okay, let me get this straight. If I trust in him, God will fill me with all—not some, but all—joy and peace? And then hope will overflow?*

It sounded so simple; almost too good to be true. But again, I had to act on it. So as best I could, I began to intentionally base my life on God's Word. I started trusting him. I went back to Isaiah 50:10 a thousand times, trusting in the Name of my Lord. His faithful, compassionate, and kind Name. To me, his best Name is, by far, Savior. For on the cross I saw the God of all hope. And in him, I have hope overflowing.

Meditate: God will fill you with
all joy and peace as you trust him.
That's his promise.

55

Amazing Love

As *knowledge* is commonly the measure of *love,*
the deeper and more extensive our *knowledge*
shall be, the greater will be our *love:* and if our
love of GOD were great we should love Him
equally in pains and pleasures.

— Brother Lawrence, page 62

Years of pain have taught me that if you want to know Christ deeply—not skating the surface but intimately—it will mean journeying through deep suffering. Think of it: When Jesus gave you his most amazing, life-transforming display of love; when he showed you the height, depth, and breadth of that love; when he withheld nothing but wrung himself inside out to death, pouring out all of his love to the last drop . . . it happened on a torturous cross, his greatest point of horror and anguish. It seems then that if we are to know Jesus in an intimate way, it will take place in our own points of horror and anguish.

Although God freely bestows his love, he's not at anyone's command. As the solemn Monarch of the universe, he shares his intimacy on his own terms. And those terms call for us to suffer and, in some measure, to suffer as his beloved Son did while on earth. We may not understand his reasons, but we are foolish to fight him on this. He is ecstasy beyond words, and it is worth anything to be his friend. Your call to suffer comes from a God tender beyond description. If you fail to remember this, you will misread him in your worst afflictions and eventually grow to hate him. Do not misinterpret the ways of your loving Lord. Learn to view your pain as your private meeting place—a hard but personal space where you will know Christ's most amazing love for you beyond a doubt.

Meditate: Earth has no sorrow
that heaven cannot heal.

56

See Him by Faith

I must, in a little time, go to GOD. What comforts me
in this life is, that I now see Him by *faith;* and I see
Him in such a manner as might make me say sometimes,
I believe no more, but I see. I feel what faith teaches us,
and in that assurance and that practice of faith,
I will live and die with Him.

—Brother Lawrence, page 56

When I paint, before I mix a single color, I carefully sketch my composition. The lines make up the firm structure on which I paint, let's say, a bowl of apples. When the painting is nearly complete, the composition virtually disappears and pure style emerges. You no longer sees lines but only apples that appear so luscious you can almost taste them. This is perhaps what Brother Lawrence meant when he wrote, "I believe no more, but I see." In painterly language, the composition and structure of his belief in Jesus emerged into a vision of Christ that was so complete, so beautiful and real, that he could almost see his Savior.

Exercising faith in Jesus is like building on a composition—you trust the precepts of his Word, which all point to Christ. Build on that composition long enough by obeying his Word and Jesus in all his glory begins to emerge. Your faith is the substance of things hoped for, and when you make a practice of fixing your eyes on your Blessed Hope, faith in him takes on a concrete reality. What emerges is a vision of your wonderful Lord. So meditate on his Word, marvel at his sacrifice, contemplate the depth of his love, and you will be changed, for "we all, with unveiled face, beholding the glory of the Lord, are being transformed into the same image from one degree of glory to another" (2 Corinthians 3:18, ESV). Behold Jesus, and you will see him as he is: so lovely, you could almost reach out and touch him.

Meditate: Fill your vision with Jesus and
your life will be his masterpiece.

57

A Great Work

We cannot escape the dangers which abound
in life, without the actual and *continual* help of GOD;
let us then pray to Him for it *continually.*

— Brother Lawrence, page 5 1

I am an imposing threat to the devil. And it's not because I write Christian books, run a global disability ministry, or knew Billy Graham on a first-name basis. None of this impresses Satan. What troubles him most is my trust in God. I think it's why he keeps turning up the heat. So I keep clinging to God, trusting that his right hand will uphold me (see Psalm 63:8). The devil is out to trip me, tempt me, and—if he could—snatch my life away. The more stalwart my faith, the fiercer the devil's attacks (I pray that my many sins will not expose me, making me easier prey).

I'm guided by the example of Nehemiah, who led the rebuilding of Jerusalem's walls. When wicked men tried to entice him away from his labor, Nehemiah replied, "I am doing a great work and cannot come" (Nehemiah 6:3, BSB). It's like saying, "You have only evil intentions, and I will not lay aside God's work to even listen to you." In the same way, when I sense the Enemy beckoning me away from God's work, I respond: "Devil, when you try to entice me that I'm being too hard on myself, that I shouldn't sweat the small stuff, or that I deserve time off from obeying God, I will *not* listen." Like Nehemiah, I know that God has assigned a great work for me to do; it is the great work of trusting him and busying my soul with heavenly concerns.

> Meditate: Are you an imposing threat
> to the Enemy? If not, you can be—
> with the continual help of God.

58

Remember His Kindness

Believe me; make immediately a holy and firm
resolution never more wilfully to forget Him.

—Brother Lawrence, page 43

An Iranian pastor and his wife escaped persecution by coming to America, but after a year she started panicking. "Can we please go back home?" she pleaded. "I'm spiritually falling asleep here!" She was being sung to sleep by Satan's bewitching lullaby that promised comfort, prosperity, and an abundance of "milk and honey." She was beginning to forget God.

There's nothing wrong with Costco conveniences and AMC Theatres. But we must never forget that we all live in houses richly stocked with goods we did not produce; we drink from wells we did not dig and eat from vineyards we did not plant. These are God's extraordinary gifts, but they come with a warning: "When you have eaten your fill in this land, be careful not to forget the LORD, who rescued you from slavery" (Deuteronomy 6:11–12, NLT). There's nothing wrong with "milk and honey," but it can be a little like Valium, making you forget God.

That's why the Lord gives lean times and hard afflictions. Not long ago I had a scare with my heart and lungs (aging with quadriplegia makes it more difficult to inhale enough oxygen). After receiving treatment, I'm now able to breathe better, and I cannot stop thanking Jesus. Every breath is a precious gift from him. My daily afflictions prevent me from lapsing into amnesia when it comes to remembering the many great kindnesses of my Savior. Practice the presence of Jesus today—and every day—by proclaiming, "Let all that I am praise the LORD; may I never forget the good things he does for me" (Psalm 103:2, NLT).

Meditate: What are the satanic lullabies that make you spiritually drowsy?

59

Continual Joy

I felt that prayer was nothing else but a sense of the presence of GOD, my soul being at that time insensible to everything but Divine love: and that when the appointed times of prayer were past, I found no difference, because I still continued with GOD, praising and blessing Him with all my might, so that I passed my life in continual joy.

— Brother Lawrence, page 21

Let everything that has breath praise the Lord

Psalm 150

I can be enjoying a glorious symphony, watching a breathtaking sunset, delighting in my backyard roses, or thanking God for his awesome creation, yet still, there will be an accompanying sorrow. Part of my sorrow is related to my paralysis and pain, which never goes away; the other part is a heart-wrenching awareness that my crucified Lord gave his life so that I might enjoy the beauties of this world. Suffering has made me hypersensitive to God's joys.

This wonderful and terrible mix of emotions—sorrow and joy—is described in 2 Corinthians 6:9–10, "Yet we live on . . . sorrowful, yet always rejoicing." In my most glad moments, the mingling of sorrow never goes away, and I would never wish it away. Our joys and sorrows are not separated like *I was joyful the last few days, but now, sorrow has taken over and I wonder when it will end so I can get rejoicing once more.* Joy and sorrow exist on a continuum. Good things and bad things are always happening simultaneously in our lives. The blending of joy and sorrow is a wonderful affirmation of who we are in Christ, a kind of litmus test that tells us, "This joy you are experiencing isn't frivolous or superficial. So be glad in that!" There are countless reasons for our hearts to break, but Jesus Christ makes even those sorrows into repositories of his deep and profound joy. The example of our lives flies in the face of those who think that Christian joy is all about comfort.

Meditate: If you are experiencing a
strange mix of joy and sorrow, you are
practicing Jesus's presence.

60

Father of Mercies

Since by His mercy He gives us still a little time, let us
begin in earnest, let us repair the lost time, let us return
with a full assurance to that FATHER of mercies,
Who is always ready to receive us affectionately.

— Brother Lawrence, page 51

A remnant of God's people had dragged themselves all the way across the desert from Babylon to Jerusalem. As they stood in the ruins of the destroyed temple amid rubble and weeds, God promised, "From this day on I will bless you" (Haggai 2:19).

That's nice for them, but what is *our* day of blessing? To paraphrase James Smith from the nineteenth century: What day will God bless you? The day you begin to seek the Lord. The day you decide to be on the Lord's side. The day you publicly and honestly profess him. The day you heartily engage in his work. The day you return from backsliding and repent of your sin before him.[16]

God's people had been freed from captivity; their chains were gone; they were home in the Promised Land. And God could hardly wait to bless them. It's the same for every Christian, and, like a captive returning to God, if we would but plead his promise to bless you, he will. If you would today put that bad habit behind you, if you would only let go of that grudge and reconcile with your friend or family member, if you would be honest in your dealings with people, if you would put behind you all sin, great or small . . . then you will enjoy peace like a river and your righteousness will dawn on others like the noonday sun. You will be like a tree planted by rivers of water, and whatever you put your hands to will prosper.

> Meditate: When God blesses you today,
> pass on that blessing to others.

61

Reach for a Song

Be not discouraged by the internal opposition
which you may find from nature in practicing the
presence of God. You must sacrifice yourself.

—Brother Lawrence, page 45

When pain puts me in constant crisis mode, I become easy prey for the Enemy. After a long season of trying to stay on top of my pain, I grow weary of fighting. But not too weary to reach for a song.

And not just any song. The lyrics must "possess enough spiritual muscle to barge into my soul and shake awake a hopeful response." It must be a hymn or worship song that raises me "onto a different plane spiritually; it must summon in me the emotional wherewithal to remember" my calling so I can push through my pain.[17] A timeless hymn, filled with deep truths about life and God, has power to press healing and strength into my tired heart. It also chases away the Enemy.

The devil hates to hear us sing to God. When the Colossians were struggling under the reign of the madman Nero, Paul ordered, "Let the Word of Christ dwell in you richly . . . singing psalms and hymns and spiritual songs" (Colossians 3:16, ESV). When the Ephesians were being threatened with torture, Paul told them to encourage "one another with psalms, hymns and spiritual songs" (Ephesians 5:19, NIV84). When you sing praise to God, you are standing in opposition to all of hell. You are proclaiming that God is with you in your darkness, comforting you through sadness, and working out his perfect will in your pain. Your most authentic songs of worship usually happen in the nighttime of your soul.

Meditate: The devil can't stand your worship songs, but God loves them. So keep singing.

62

On Receiving

I foresee that you will tell me that I am very much at my ease, that I eat and drink at the table of the Lord. You have reason to believe that: but think you that it would be a small pain to the greatest criminal in the world, to eat at the king's table, and be served by him, and yet have no assurance of pardon? I believe he would feel exceeding great uneasiness, and such uneasiness as nothing could alleviate, but only his trust in the goodness of his sovereign.

—Brother Lawrence, page 55

Consider the telling scene in Matthew 19:14–16. The Lord found himself amid a gaggle of kids, and he *blessed* them, bouncing little ones on his knee and tousling their hair. Seeing the disciples somewhat miffed, Jesus said,

> "Let the little children come to me, and do not hinder them, for the kingdom of heaven belongs to such as these." . . .
>
> Just then a man came up to Jesus and asked, "Teacher, what good thing must I do to get eternal life?"

Perhaps this rich young man had watched Jesus blessing the children and felt indignant that the great Teacher would lavish salvation on kids with threadbare playclothes and snotty noses. So he asked, "Teacher, what good thing must I do to get eternal life?"

It's curious how a single word can reveal the deepest motives of the heart. This young man of great wealth gave himself away with that little word *get*. "What good thing must I do to *get*?" he asked Jesus. No wonder he went away disappointed! He was all about doing something good in order to get something great. He did not realize that it was Jesus who did something good in order to give him something great—eternal life in him. Salvation is about *receiving,* not *getting.* "What can Jesus do for me?" is not the question to ask. Instead, you simply open your hands to receive mercy. Not because you've done anything to earn it but because God did everything to give it.

Meditate: Today, don't ask, "What can Jesus do for me?"
Tell him what you'll do for his kingdom.

63

Benchmarks of Grace

When outward business diverts me a little from
the thought of GOD, a fresh remembrance coming from
GOD invests my soul, and so inflames and transports
me that it is difficult for me to contain myself.

— Brother Lawrence, page 17

P ain often keeps me up at night. Not long ago, my usual sleep position was not working, and I lay wide awake. On such nights, I strengthen myself in the Lord by reciting the words to hymns, praying for other people in pain, and whispering the words of Scripture. This particular night I recited Isaiah 40:31 over and over: "Those who wait for the LORD shall renew their strength, they shall mount up with wings like eagles, they shall run and not be weary, they shall walk and not faint" (NRSV). Eventually, I fell asleep.

In the morning when my friend pulled back the drapes, she gasped and stepped away from the bay window. There perched on my small birdbath was a massive hawk. His talons clutched the rim, he arched and ruffled his feathers, and we marveled at the awesome creature, sitting serenely, a picture of supreme beauty and breathtaking power. After my harrowing night, how precious of God to gift me with "strength in the morning." It was a tangible reminder that as we wait on him, yes, he gives us grace aplenty to mount up on wings like a hawk, if not an eagle. When we open the eyes of our hearts, God will always surprise us with benchmarks of his grace. I suppose if God can direct a whale underwater to swallow Jonah, he can direct a huge hawk to greet me at the start of a new day. How did Jesus greet you this morning? What vivid reminders has he given you of his favor?

Meditate: Ask God to open the eyes of your
heart to see evidences of his care.

64

The Narrow Way

We should establish ourselves in a sense of
GOD's Presence, by continually conversing with Him.
That it is a shameful thing to quit His conversation,
to think of trifles and fooleries.

That we should feed and nourish our souls
with high notions of GOD; which would yield us
great joy in being devoted to Him.

— Brother Lawrence, page 8

In Matthew 7:13, Jesus said, "Enter through the narrow gate. For wide is the gate and broad is the road that leads to destruction, and many enter through it." Was Jesus only referring to being born again? No. Here, Jesus is talking to *me,* one of his ardent disciples! And if you are a believer, he is speaking to you too. His point is broader than just salvation.

Yes, Christians *are* justified by faith and are secure in Christ, but when Jesus says, "Strive to enter through the narrow door," he's talking about a way of life for his loved ones (Luke 13:24, ESV). I want to be content and happy in Christ, so I strive for the narrow way. I dare not become complacent or allow myself to think, *Let me see how close I can get to this sinful behavior without it becoming a habit.* Or, *I wonder how long I can watch this mindless TV program without it dampening my spirit?* Right there, I'm already on the broad way that leads to destruction—a destruction of my sensitivity to the Spirit's touch and voice as well as a dismantling of my interest in heavenly things. There are many on that road to destruction, but Jesus calls his followers to enter the narrow way, to strive for the narrow door. So we do the hard work of striving to find our peace and joy in Jesus Christ. For when we have contentment in him, we won't be interested in tiptoeing near foolish behavior.

Meditate: In what ways can you sharpen your hearing for when the Spirit speaks?

65

An Instrument of Mercy

I have been often near expiring, though I was
never so much satisfied as then. Accordingly I did not
pray for any relief, but I prayed for strength to
suffer with courage, humility, and love. Ah, how
sweet is it to suffer with GOD! however great
the sufferings may be, receive them with love.

— Brother Lawrence, page 60

P anic *consumed* me after I broke my neck. While my friends went off to college or landed jobs, I stayed stuck in a hospital. Life felt bleak, and I wanted someone to magically promise that everything would be okay.

It's the heartfelt plea of all who suffer. We want assurance that somehow things will work out in the end. We want to know that our world is orderly and stable, not spinning off into nightmarish chaos. We want God to be at the center of our suffering, not only holding our lives together but holding *us*. Like a father who picks up his crying child, pats him on his back, and says, "There, there, honey, everything will be okay. Daddy's here." That's our plea; we want God to be Daddy.

In Romans 8:28 we have the massive promise of that very assurance: "And we know that for those who love God all things work together for good, for those who are called according to his purpose" (ESV). Here our Abba Father tells us he is so in charge of everything that all hard things are ordered to serve our ultimate good. This is true whether we face tribulation, distress, persecution, famine, nakedness, peril, or sword. It's true whether we face broken homes, broken hearts, or broken necks. The robust hope of the believer is not that we will escape a long list of bad things, but that God will make every one of our agonies an instrument of his mercy to do us good—in the here and now and in the hereafter.

Meditate: Ask God to reveal the good things
he is doing through today's trials.

66

Join the Dance

Let all our business be to *know* GOD:
the more one *knows* Him, the more
one desires to *know* Him.

—Brother Lawrence, page 62

God is love. He is not a threatened, pacing deity starving for attention. He does not bite his nails or blow his stack. Far from it. God is "the blessed and only Ruler, the King of kings and Lord of lords" (1 Timothy 6:15). One translation reads "the blissful God."[18] Scan the Bible's big picture, and you'll find that he's rapturously happy. The nature of such Love is to overflow onto another (love requires someone to love, right?). God the Father pours out his love on Jesus the Son because the Father's own perfections are flawlessly reflected there. Jesus is God the Father standing in the mirror. In Jesus, God sees the fountain of all the intelligence, grandeur, and goodness that ever was. We look in the mirror and are almost always disappointed, but God looks in the mirror and is riveted. The mutual love between the Father and the Son is so rich, full, and forceful that it swirls in a glorious and powerful dance orchestrated by the Holy Spirit. The eternal Trinity revels together in a swirling ballet of mutual love.

I want to join that dance. So I whisper, "Jesus, you are so much better than anything I had planned on my feet. You are far more fulfilling than life as I once liked it. My old life was loaded with shiny trinkets, not to be compared with the joy of knowing you. Thank you for inviting me into your happiness!"

Meditate: Join the dance today!
Delight yourself in the love of God.

67

In His Presence

Let it be *your* business to keep your mind in the presence
of the LORD: if it sometimes wander, withdraw itself from
Him, do not much disquiet yourself for that.

—*Brother Lawrence, page 49*

It was a rainy Saturday, and I was working at my computer when it froze. My paralyzed hands couldn't press the reset. My voice activation wasn't helpful either. A tray table blocked my way, so I couldn't wheel outside to get my husband. I yelled for him, but it was useless. I sat quietly for a few minutes; then, sensing self-pity on the rise, I chose a different path. I remembered in whose presence I sat. I knew, somehow, that what I did with that moment would count for all eternity.

So while rain spattered outside, I recalled all the things I so easily take for granted. I recited, "I am a co-heir with Christ, and one day all my labors will be rewarded. I am his bride, and one day his joy will flood my heart to overflowing. I am a citizen of heaven where self-pity, sadness, and sin will vanish. I shall be swept up in the love of God, carried along on a wild and wonderful current of impossible pleasure. One day, these paralyzed hands and legs will rise and work, and I will jump up and shout, 'I knew it would be good but not *this* good!'"

My spirit was coming up! God was giving me buckets of grace with every victorious statement of who I am in Jesus Christ. So whatever challenges you face, I encourage you to rehearse your identity and destiny often and say aloud: "I keep my eyes always on the LORD. With him at my right hand, I will not be shaken. Therefore my heart is glad. . . . You will fill me with joy in your presence, with eternal pleasures at your right hand" (Psalm 16:8–9, 11).

Meditate: Are your spirits low?
Rehearse aloud who you are in Jesus Christ.

68

No More Wrath

I commonly employed myself during the time set apart for devotion and prayer, with the thoughts of death, judgment, hell, heaven, and my sins. Thus I continued some years applying my mind carefully the rest of the day, and even in the midst of my work, *to the presence of* GOD, Whom I considered always as *with* me, often as *in* me.

—Brother Lawrence, pages 30–31

C hristian culture nowadays rarely mentions judgment, hell, or even heaven. Rarer still is talk about sin. But examining these things is essential if we arc to understand why Jesus came. For the God who hated sin in the Old Testament—and hated it with all the fire and brimstone he could muster—is the same God who still hates sin in the New Testament. Yet the difference is the way God expresses his wrath. Leaf through Matthew, Mark, Luke, and John and you will never see God's wrath breaking out through plagues, earthquakes, fire, or brimstone. Instead, it breaks out on Calvary.

All the white-hot rage that God had stored up for our sins against his nature and our neighbors was poured out on his own Son. There at the cross, Jesus carried every plague, pestilence, stoning, and snake-infested drought; every hailstorm, invasion of locusts, enslavement by enemy forces, and unthinkable cruelty perpetrated by vicious Assyrians and Babylonians. Jesus took it all, willingly.

God has no more wrath left for you and me, only mercy and lovingkindness if we would but trust Christ as Lord and Savior. Not a day goes by that I don't thank Jesus for taking the blow intended for me! "For God made Christ, who never sinned, to be the offering for our sin, so that we could be made right with God through Christ" (2 Corinthians 5:21, NLT).

Meditate: Live in a manner worthy of what Jesus did on the cross.

69

The Crown of God's Creation

In our conversations with GOD,
we are also employed in praising, adoring,
and loving Him incessantly, for His infinite
goodness and perfection.

— Brother Lawrence, page 20

My husband, Ken, and I recently took a trip to Yosemite National Park, famous for its ancient, giant sequoias, astonishingly high waterfalls, and granite monoliths like El Capitan and Half Dome. Ken rented a bicycle, and he wheeled alongside me as we breezed by rivers, meadows, and pristine lakes. As we wheeled the paths, the stunning scenery around us inspired constant praise of Jesus (we wondered how many park visitors were also thinking of him).

One of the reasons God created the landscape now preserved in that iconic park was so that its visitors might be stirred spiritually, gaze up at El Capitan, and ask, "Who is the Creator behind such astounding beauty?" For

> what may be known about God is plain to [everyone], because God has made it plain to them. For since the creation of the world God's invisible qualities—his eternal power and divine nature—have been clearly seen, being understood from what has been made. (Romans 1:19–20)

Creation is ours to enjoy, so we should savor it—but I'm certain Jesus takes greater delight in his followers when they pray for the crown of God's creation, such as the people on the park trams and at the kiosks and at the bike rental store. For all of Yosemite's world-renowned beauty, it cannot hold a candle to the epitome of God's creation: human beings. "God saw that it was good" when he created the earth and all that is in it, but after he made man and woman, "God saw all that he had made, and it was *very* good" (Genesis 1:31).

Meditate: Your family and friends are the epitome of God's creation. Treat them well.

70

Jesus Is the Answer

I worshipped Him the oftenest that I could,
keeping my mind in His holy Presence, and recalling
it as often as I found it wandered from Him. . . . I made
this my business, as much all the day long as
at the appointed times of prayer; for at all times,
every hour, every minute, even in the height of my
business, I drove away from my mind everything that
was capable of interrupting my thought of GOD.

—Brother Lawrence, page 28

There was once a season when I was so overwhelmed by chronic pain that I almost became blind to God's offer of enabling grace. Pain has a way of heightening our natural inclinations to doubt God. But in Christ we have transcendent inclinations, for we are called to live supernaturally. We can live hopefully. Miraculously. Powerfully. So I let my pain drive me back to the book of Job and saw that despite his blinding afflictions, Job never turned away from God. At the height of his suffering, Job cried out after the Lord, "If only I knew where to find him; if only I could go to his dwelling! I would state my case before him. . . . I would find out what he would answer me, and consider what he would say to me" (23:3–5).

Job turned *to* God, not *away* from him. It is a powerful lesson for us. We even have an advantage over Job. For when we are steeped in suffering, we don't need to wonder where to find God; he is found in Christ. God does not dwell far away; rather, we say "Christ lives in me" (Galatians 2:20). Like Job, we might state our case before God, but Jesus is already at God's side, pleading our cause and working as our Advocate (see 1 John 2:1). And if, like Job, we are looking for answers, we've already found them—God gave his best and only Answer at the cross. Today, live hopefully, miraculously, and powerfully, for Christ has the final word when it comes to your suffering. Jesus is your Answer, so practice his presence in your suffering.

Meditate: God owes us no explanations.
He explained enough on the cross.

71

The Fountain of Life

Let us seek Him often by faith:
He is within us; seek Him not elsewhere.

— *Brother Lawrence, pages 62–63*

If I want to keep my quadriplegic body in good health, I must drink water every morning, afternoon, and evening. I cannot take shortcuts and consume the required amount all at once, let's say, in the morning. My body, for lack of exercise, needs continuous cleansing and renewal. And so does my spirit. Throughout the day, tiny rebellions clutter and clog my soul, and I must flush them out.

Years ago I memorized Psalm 63, and virtually every morning before dawn, I use it to prime my pump for the Living Water. Lying awake, I tell Jesus, "You, God, are my God, earnestly I seek you; I thirst for you, my whole being longs for you, in a dry and parched land where there is no water" (Psalm 63:1). I pray, "Fill me up, God. Fill me to the fullest because today I will leak. And leak badly." Just as buckets leak, gas tanks empty, flowers dry out, and birdbaths evaporate, my spirit withers quicker than I realize. Even when I may not feel thirsty for Christ, I am aware that my soul is prone to dry up and become brittle. Jesus says in John 7:37, "Let anyone who is thirsty come to me and drink." That's me! And I dare not risk losing my taste for him. Jesus doesn't *have* what my soul needs; he *is* what I need. Drink from his greatness, for you were made to live on him. Throughout your day, flush and refresh your spirit with frequent drinks from the Fountain of Life.

Meditate: Seek God frequently throughout
the day and be refreshed.

72

Remain in Him

How can we pray to Him without being with Him?
How can we be with Him but in thinking of Him often?
And how can we often think of Him, but by a holy habit
which we should form of it? You will tell me that I am
always saying the same thing: it is true, for this is
the best and easiest method I know; and as I use
no other, I advise all the world to it.

— Brother Lawrence, page 51

People often comment on how strong I must be. But here's the thing: I am *not* a strong person, so I'm always calling on Jesus for help. I am feeble and needy, so I'm constantly praying that he'll keep my poor soul from straying and keep me moving forward through pain. I need Jesus so urgently, I sometimes wonder if he was thinking of me when he said, "Whoever eats my flesh and drinks my blood remains in me, and I in them" (John 6:56). Far from being gross, these words are my meat and drink. I hunger and thirst after him. Remaining in Jesus is *that* intimate.

Later in the gospel of John, Jesus used another metaphor to illustrate the intimacy of "remaining in him." He said, "I am the vine; you are the branches. . . . Apart from me you can do nothing" (John 15:5). The vine and its branches are one and the same, not separate. We cannot disengage from the Vine and then graft ourselves back into him when we need him. Remaining in Christ is not like plugging yourself into a power source until your spiritual batteries read 100 percent. It doesn't work that way. A healthy relationship with Jesus is an abiding one. Remaining in him is not sporadic or occasional, like popping in on a good friend when you need his help. So be the branch that rests in the vine. "Eat his flesh and drink his blood" as though your spiritual veins were his. Be that close, that intimate. For without him, we are nothing.

Meditate: Be intimate with God today.
Give him your thirsty soul.

73

Satisfaction

I cannot imagine how religious persons can
live satisfied without the practice of *the presence of* GOD.
For my part I keep myself retired with Him in the . . .
centre of my soul as much as I can.

—Brother Lawrence, page 44

E veryone wants to be satisfied with their lives, but if you make satisfaction your aim, it's the one thing you'll never have. Only when we seek God are we truly satisfied. I can tell I am most satisfied in Jesus when I have that settled sense of being firmly fixed in him, unmovable and unshakable. Like he's my home base. My fulcrum on which everything balances. The plumb line that makes everything straight. The center of my solar system around which everything orbits. Satisfaction is finding shade and shelter in the "one God . . . who is over all and through all and in all" (Ephesians 4:6).

Why would I ever want to drift away from such a Savior? But, like everyone, I am prone to wander. Which is why I make Psalm 73:28 my anchor: "It is good to be near God. I have made the Sovereign LORD my refuge." It is not good for me to wander any distance from God (the previous verse warns, "Those who are far from you will perish"). I must not risk that, so I stay near God and "make the Lord my refuge." I don't draw near him to fathom his mysterious ways concerning my suffering or to get clarity on his purpose for my life. I draw near to find refuge, shelter, sanctuary, and a safe harbor. Resting in his shadow, I am back on home base. I am *satisfied* and "will say of the LORD, 'He is my refuge . . . my God, in whom I trust' " (Psalm 91:2).

Meditate: How would you describe
being satisfied in Christ?

74

Celebrate the Victories

Use yourself then by degrees thus to worship Him,
to beg His grace, to offer Him your heart from time to time,
in the midst of your business, even every moment if you
can. Do not always scrupulously confine yourself to certain
rules, or particular forms of devotion; but act with a general
confidence in GOD, with love and humility.

— *Brother Lawrence, page 47*

Throughout the rhythms of my day, I talk to Jesus in snippets. My first sip of morning coffee lifts an aroma of pleasant thoughts toward him. The side door opens, my eyes rest on the backyard rosebush, and I tell Jesus how ingenious he is with color. I wheel outside for a midday break, feel the breeze, and thank him that his Spirit touches me the same way.

Practicing Jesus adoration—sixty seconds at a time—is a discipline that corrals me close to him throughout the day. Do the same and do it often: sing the stanza of a hymn to God, memorize a short Bible verse, covenant with yourself to bless the Lord every time you see a stunning sunset. Yesterday evening, I lingered by our bay window, and as the sunset faded, I called for Ken to snap a photo. We drank in the golden glow stretching beyond the mountains. Purples and pinks kept shifting as the sun dropped below the hills and . . . we worshiped. In return, God gave us Amy Carmichael's timeless words, "We shall have all eternity to celebrate the victories, but we have only the few hours before sunset in which to win them."[19] The few hours of this life are quickly passing, so be mindful to acknowledge God-sent moments that are infused with heaven. They are his tender taps on your shoulder.

Meditate: Break free of your quiet-time routine — find fresh ways to adore Jesus today.

75

Proof of His Love

I am in pain to see you suffer so long:
what gives me some ease, and sweetens the
feeling I have of your griefs is, that they are proofs of
GOD's love towards you: see them in that view,
and you will bear them more easily.

— Brother Lawrence, page 58

There is no doubt that Jesus deeply loved Mary, Martha, and Lazarus. They were dear friends who were precious in his sight—holy and beloved by him (see Isaiah 43:4; Colossians 3:12). These three were, well, Jesus's favorites. But as deeply as he loved them, Jesus dealt them tragedy, disappointment, and death. My point? If you are close to the Lord, do not assume he will spare you from severe suffering.

That's because the core of Christ's plan is to rescue us from our sin and restore us to abundant life. Our tragedies and disappointments are not his ultimate focus. He cares about them, but they are merely symptoms of the real problem. Jesus cares most not about making us comfortable but about teaching us to hate our sins, grow up spiritually, and love him. To do this, he gives us salvation's benefits only gradually, sometimes painfully so. Jesus allows you (and Mary, Martha, and Lazarus) to feel much of sin's sting while we're heading for heaven. This constantly reminds us of what we're being delivered from and exposes sin for the poison it is. Evil (suffering) is turned on its head to defeat another kind of evil (sin)—all to the praise of God's wisdom. Jesus hung on a cross so that his dearly beloved would *never* have to suffer hell, not so that they wouldn't suffer here on earth. No one goes to Christ's heaven who doesn't first share in Christ's sufferings. It is a proof that they belong to Jesus.

Meditate: What good things are you
gaining through affliction?

76

An Expanded Vision

People observed, that in the greatest hurry of business in the kitchen, I still preserved my recollection of God and heavenly-mindedness. I tried never to be hasty, nor loiter, but I tried to do each thing in its season, with an even uninterrupted composure and tranquillity of spirit.

The time of business does not with me differ from the time of prayer; and in the noise and clutter of my kitchen, while several persons are at the same time calling for different things, I possess GOD in as great tranquillity as if I were upon my knees before God and heaven.

— *Brother Lawrence, page 26*

Nehemiah was a cupbearer for King Artaxerxes. When Nehemiah learned that the walls of Jerusalem were in ruins, he said, "I sat down and wept. For some days I mourned and fasted and prayed before the God of heaven" (1:4). Then he offered up an ambitious prayer for Jerusalem's walls to be rebuilt. At the close of his lengthy petition, he added a postscript: "I was cupbearer to the king" (1:11). Nehemiah had it in his heart to build big walls, but saw himself as a lowly cupbearer.

He then spent four more months in prayer before he asked the king for permission to go back to Jerusalem. The king noticed his sad countenance and asked him what he wanted, but before Nehemiah replied, he prayed again (see 2:4). I find it remarkable that God's man had already spent months in prayer yet felt the need for more prayer before he spoke. It's also noteworthy that those weeks of praise and petition expanded Nehemiah's vision and confidence—he no longer saw himself as a cupbearer. Now Nehemiah saw himself as a restorer of cities. He asks Artaxerxes to let him go rebuild the walls of Jerusalem, a request that could have sent a servant to the gallows (see 2:5).

Prayer had turned Nehemiah into a man of great vision. Do you lack courage, confidence, and vision? Spend significant time in prayer, and you'll be amazed at who you can be in Christ.

Meditate: Ask God to show you his kingdom vision and how you can be a part of it!

77

He Goes with You

I know that to arrive at this state of consolation
about our illness, the beginning is very difficult; for we must
act purely in faith. But though it is difficult, we know also
that we can do all things with the grace of GOD, which He
never refuses to them who ask it earnestly.

—Brother Lawrence, page 61

After the accident in which I became paralyzed, I was terrified of the future. If only God would give me some assurance that everything would turn out okay, then I could trust him.

My concerns were not unlike those of Moses. After God's people rebelled, the Lord told Moses to get up and lead the people beyond the desert to Canaan. Moses, being a little unsure of what lay ahead, said to the Lord, "You have been telling me, 'Take these people up to the Promised Land.' . . . If it is true that you look favorably on me, let me know your ways so I may understand you more fully" (Exodus 33:12–13, NLT). In other words, "Lord, let me know what you have in mind, what you intend to do, and how it will all work out. Then I will be happy to lead your people." The Lord simply replied, "I will personally go with you, Moses" (Exodus 33:14, NLT). That's it? Moses was hoping for details, a plan, the blueprint. He wanted assurance about the future.

When God gives *us* a directive, before venturing out, we want to know what he intends to do. "Let me know the way you're taking me, God." But God does not unfold the blueprint; he *is* the blueprint. If we are insistent in wanting to know the way, let's recall that Jesus *is* the Way. Once I started powering my wheelchair into the future, I could almost hear the words from Exodus: "I will personally go with you, Joni." And for more than half a century, he has.

Meditate: Worried about the future?
His presence is all you need. Thank him for that.

78

Constant Devotion

Make immediately a holy and firm resolution never
more wilfully to forget Him, and to spend the rest of
your days in His sacred presence, deprived for the
love of Him, if He thinks fit, of all consolations.

— Brother Lawrence, page 43

I don't want to wait for heaven for my heart to overflow with constant devotion to Jesus. I want a big heart for him *now*. So rather than lean toward earthly things, I run to the things of heaven. I say to God, "I shall run the way of Your commandments, for You will enlarge my heart" (Psalm 119:32, NASB). I long for a roomy, more spacious heart for God. Like the old Puritan Richard Baxter, I keep pushing my heart into the presence of Jesus:

> Take your heart once again and lead it by the hand. . . . Show it the kingdom of Christ and the glory of it. Say to your heart, "All this will your Lord bestow on you. . . . This is your own inheritance! This crown is yours. These pleasures are yours. This beauteous place is yours. All things are yours, because you are Christ's and Christ is yours." . . .
>
> Hold out a little longer, oh my soul, and bear with the infirmities of your earthly tabernacle, for soon you will rest from all your afflictions. . . .
>
> Be up and doing; run, strive, fight, and hold on, for you have a certain glorious prize before you.[20]

Believers who are content to know little of God are usually content with a small devotion toward him. I cannot settle for that. I keep yielding my heart's hidden chambers to the Spirit. I busy my heart with new affections for my Savior. Why shouldn't my heart be set on Jesus Christ, when so much of his heart is set on me?

Meditate: In what ways can you better manage your heart?

79

Idols Never Satisfy

The practice of the presence of God does not much fatigue the body: it is, however, proper to deprive it sometimes, nay often, of many little pleasures which are innocent and lawful: for GOD will not permit that a soul which desires to be devoted entirely to Him, should take other pleasures than with Him.

—Brother Lawrence, page 44

My friend Diana struggled for many years with an unhealthy weight. She wrote, "Joni, for decades I have clung to the 'worthless idol' of food addiction to temporarily soothe all of the pain and stresses of my life." Well, Diana did something about that worthless idol. She stopped feeding her addiction and has lost more than ninety pounds! What inspired her? Jonah 2:8: "Those who cling to worthless idols forfeit the grace that could be theirs" (NIV84).

When we succumb to pleasures that do us damage, we forfeit grace; that is, the divine power to live as we should. Christ has a daily storehouse of his favor, strength, patience, pleasure, endurance, abundant joy, supernatural insight, miraculous provision, and providential timing, but we forfeit all of it when we prefer our idols. What idols? It could be TV, computer games, people's assessment of you, sports, Instagram, marital status, alcohol, social position, certain relationships, or even a big plate of cookies. When we tell ourselves we "cannot live without that person" or "cannot do without this" or "must have that," we are idolaters.

If I keep feeding my fleshly appetites, my soul will reflect those same low, selfish pursuits. If my heart is captivated by the beauties of Christ, my soul will reflect that same greatness. *That's* what I want. My better angels tell me that idols can't hold a candle to the matchless worth of Jesus. Today, loosen your grip on "must-have" things and people, and discover a reservoir of sweet, enabling favor in Christ.

Meditate: When you cling to an idol,
you diminish your soul, becoming less
than you could and should be.

80

Innumerable Consolations

Love sweetens pains; and when one loves GOD,
one suffers for His sake with joy and courage.
Do you so, I ask of you; comfort yourself with Him,
Who is the only Physician of all our maladies.

—*Brother Lawrence, page 59*

The Lord is delighted to call himself "the God of all comfort" (2 Corinthians 1:3). He does not supply merely a little comfort, or some comfort, but all that heaven can muster for your need. He offers you innumerable consolations through countless channels. One way is never good enough for God—he floods his comfort toward you through a thousand tributaries, seeking to support you where it hurts the most. I know this because I have experienced it.

When you are wounded, it's hard to find more personal words than Isaiah 46:4; God speaks here not through a prophet or some other messenger, but one-on-one with you, saying tenderly, "I am he, I am he who will sustain you. I have made you and I will carry you; I will sustain you and I will rescue you." It's a promise; he *will* sustain you. God stakes his character on it.

Perhaps the most heartwarming expression of God's comfort is in Isaiah 49:16. Look at your Savior's hands and hear him say, "See, I have written your name on the palms of my hands" (NLT). When the Son of God engraves our names in his "flesh," it is much more than *Joni, Ken, Bobby,* or *Jessica.* It's everything your name represents. If he has carved your many pains and concerns into his palm, will he not care for your tiniest problems? He has etched each one into himself! He has more compassion for your frailties than you could ever imagine.

Meditate: God engages his whole being
in sustaining and comforting you.

81

Turn Your Soul

There is not in the world a kind of life more
sweet and delightful, than that of a continual conversation
with GOD: those only can comprehend it who practise
and experience it: yet I do not advise you to do it from
that motive; it is not pleasure which we ought to
seek in this exercise; but let us do it from a principle
of love, and because GOD would have us.

— Brother Lawrence, pages 42–43

Occasionally, the misery of paralysis and unending pain makes prayer feel impossible—like I'm stretching for the stars. Even when I muster the strength to pray, the mumbled words feel heartless, messy, and meandering. Aha! But my breathing is consistent. It is steady and reliable and a gift from God. So I set it apart as a prayer, consecrating it and lacing it with words when possible. Breathing is the outpouring of my very life in its simplest form. It's the most fundamental and irreplaceable act of the human experience, and I sanctify it when I direct it toward heaven. My paralysis may drain me of power, but it is not only what I say that reaches God; it is also the turning of my soul upward that reaches him. It is the lifting of my head and, yes, my breath to heaven. Suffering may push me down, but it cannot keep me from rising. No matter how hard it flattens me, I can lift my very being—my breath—toward heaven.

If it were my gossamer breath alone, however, it would fail on its path to heaven. I have consecrated that breath, and so my tiny prayers find a willing friend on their way to the stars. God is friendly toward my heaven-sent inclinations, even my breath prayers, because they are hallowed and sealed by the blood of Christ. Therefore, I know God will hear and accept my most fainthearted gift of quiet submission, breathed in and out.

Meditate: Keep turning your soul toward God "for in him we live and move and have our being" (Acts 17:28).

82

Appreciate His Blessings

When sometimes I had not thought of GOD
for a good while, I was not upset by it. But after having
acknowledged my wretchedness to GOD, I returned
to Him with so much the greater trust in Him.

— Brother Lawrence, pages 16–17

We Christians are like fish swimming in a cultural ocean of entitlement—our society has stripped personal rights of their biblical foundation, so any discussion of rights is now a haranguing competition to prove who is the most victimized. This can't help but breed division and suspicion. Sadly, our minds have become saturated by this self-focused worldview. We want a God who will support our plans—one on whom we can project our wants and wishes. We make God our accomplice: someone we can rely on as long as he's doing our bidding. If God does something bizarre, we keep him in our vocabulary but discreetly click "unsubscribe" and quietly unfriend him.

Christians are "crucified with Christ"; we are dead to ourselves (Galatians 2:20). We have no rights, so we are not entitled to anything. Thus, when Jesus chooses to bless us with good health, comfort, ease, or security, we are indeed grateful, but we are also wise as serpents. We realize how easily we can fashion these blessings into idols. In God's scheme of things, no one is entitled. As soon as we come to Jesus, his Spirit starts transforming our minds, warning us,

> Don't let the world around you squeeze you into its own mould, but let God re-mould your minds from within, so that you may prove in practice that the plan of God for you is good, meets all his demands and moves towards the goal of true maturity. (Romans 12:2, PHILLIPS)

Meditate: Practice the presence of Jesus by dying to all your personal rights and receiving blessings as the glorious gifts they are!

83

God Is for You

The apprehension that I was not devoted to GOD, as I wished to be, my past sins always present to my mind, and the great unmerited favours which GOD did me were the matter and source of my sufferings. During this time I fell often, and rose again presently. It seemed to me that the creatures, reason, and GOD Himself were against me; and *faith* alone for me.

—Brother Lawrence, pages 31–32

When I read this statement by Brother Lawrence, I respond,

> What, then, shall we say in response to these things? If God is for us, who can be against us? He who did not spare his own Son, but gave him up for us all— how will he not also, along with him, graciously give us all things? (Romans 8:31–32)

Yes, I sin, but God is still for me. He is so much "for me" that his Son stayed pierced through on his cross until every vestige of my sin was paid for. God spared Abraham's beloved son by telling Abraham not to thrust the knife into his boy's chest . . . but God didn't spare his Boy. God killed Jesus because it was the only way he could avoid killing you and me.

God will certainly, without any doubt or possibility of failure, "graciously give us all things." Often I lie in bed at night recounting the "all things" he gives me—like courage, joy, hope, and peace. I have the guarantee that whatever heinous thing may oppose me, it will surely fail. Demons may rush at me with their battering rams, but all their assaults amount to nothing. Their threats even turn out to be a benefit to me; Almighty God promises to take every pressure and pain, strip it of its damaging power to my soul, and give me healing power in its place. I strengthen myself with these reminders. For whatever else may disappoint me, whatever else fails and gives way, this will never, ever give way: God is for me.

Meditate: How is God graciously giving you all things?

84

A Step of Faith

It is, however, necessary to put our whole trust in GOD, laying aside all other cares, and even some particular forms of devotion, though very good in themselves, yet such as one often engages in unreasonably: because those devotions are only means to attain to the end; so when by this exercise of *the presence of* GOD we are *with Him* Who is our end.

— Brother Lawrence, page 45

Once I was backing my wheelchair out of my van on a steep incline. It was scary. The van was tilted, which made the ramp even steeper. Ken was behind me, holding on to the handles of my chair, saying, "It's okay, Joni, I've got you!" I had my doubts. Yet others were watching us, which meant I had to make a choice. I could either make my husband look good by trusting him and blindly backing out of the van, or I could make him look careless and untrustworthy by refusing to budge. Whatever I decided would prove what I thought about Ken's character and my confidence in his word.

I had that same decision when I broke my neck. I had big doubts about God's purpose and plan, and I wasn't certain he could be trusted. I had a choice. I could either make God look good by trusting him and blindly wheeling into a life of paralysis, or I could make him look bad by insisting he was unfair. I could either glorify his reputation or stain it. My decision would prove to everyone looking on what I believed about God and the reliability of his Word. In the end, I took a step of faith and placed my future in his hands. I've never regretted it.

The best thing you can do for yourself, as well as for the people around you, is to trust God. The harder things are, the better you make God look when you put your faith in him.

Meditate: Make Jesus look magnificent today.
Trust him!

85

Worthy of the Gospel

I was very aware of my faults, but not discouraged by them;
that I confessed them to GOD, and did not plead against
Him to excuse them. When I had done so, I peaceably
resumed my usual practice of love and adoration.

—Brother Lawrence, page 14

Because I'm a Christian, God has given me a new nature with a bent toward pleasing Jesus. At the same time, I'm still a sinner who possesses a bent toward using my own conduct as my standard of virtue. I easily measure my righteousness by my own good behavior, by how merciful, grateful, and generous I think I am. Every Christian struggles with this, for when we judge ourselves by ourselves, we easily become convinced that we're doing okay and living as we should. Mercy, gratitude, generosity, and a whole list of other virtues become "ours," as though they originate from within our good character. Not so. Rather, "You are my Lord; apart from you I have no good thing" (Psalm 16:2). This is why God tells us to conduct ourselves in a manner worthy of the gospel (see Philippians 1:27). For then, we are looking into the perfect mirror of God's law. When the gospel is our focus, we see ourselves accurately for the first time.

If you want to get a true assessment of your virtues and your faults, then delve into what the gospel requires of you. Then, as Philippians 1:27 says, whatever happens, you will be better equipped to honestly and humbly respond in a manner worthy of the gospel. Pretense aside, you will be ready to practice the love of Jesus.

Meditate: "I say to the LORD, 'You are my Lord; apart from you I have no good thing'" (Psalm 16:2).

86

The Little Remembrance

Lift up your heart to Him, sometimes even
at your meals, and when you are in company:
the least little remembrance will always be
acceptable to Him.

—Brother Lawrence, page 46

It was early morning, and my helper Crystal was busy giving me a bed bath, stretching my limbs, and putting on my corset. While she worked, I struggled to greet the day, having slept poorly the night before due to intense pain. Our talk centered on day-to-day routines, including a new pressure area on my hip and what seemed to be a clogged bladder catheter. Everything felt dull and ordinary until, out of the blue, she remarked offhandedly, "Isn't Jesus good, keeping you so healthy for all that you do?" Suddenly, my spirit stood at attention and my soul aligned with the sunny morning. Crystal had spoken words of life.

Proverbs 18:21 says, "The tongue has the power of life and death, and those who love it will eat its fruit." Although people will one day have to eat the fruit of their damaging and hurtful words, others like Crystal will be gloriously recompensed for their uplifting words. That morning, my helper unwittingly did a great deal of good to herself and to me, and one day she will be rewarded for it. Charles Spurgeon wrote,

> Our tongue is the glory of our frame, and it is given us that we may give glory to him who framed it. Articulate speech, which is denied to birds and beasts, is given to us for this major reason—that we may articulately and distinctly praise and magnify the name of the Most High.[21]

God tells us in Isaiah 57:19, "I create the fruit of the lips; Peace, peace" (KJV). We are created to breathe life-giving words of hope and peace, just as Crystal did . . . almost without thinking.

Meditate: Be bold. Be intentional.
Little words of life go far.

87

Transcending the Ordinary

I need neither art nor science for going to GOD,
but only a heart resolutely determined
to apply itself to nothing but Him, or for
His sake, and to love Him only.

—Brother Lawrence, page 19

I love to create watercolors and oil paintings. As a painter, I have long believed that secular culture cannot explain why beautiful things matter. It has lost the meaning of beauty and lost touch with reality, especially spiritual reality beyond the material world. Today, our culture denies the supreme Creator, Jesus Christ, and instead, embraces a fascination with ugliness. This filth fills our museums and speaks through movies, popular music, and books. The art of today—so lauded by critics—might be dead animals in a tank, piles of trash, or urinals. To call such things "art" doesn't just rob the word of meaning; it robs our world of meaning.

Beauty reminds us as nothing else can that there is much more to life than merely functioning in a material world. Beauty carries us to higher, more noble, and exalted things. When you hear a stirring concerto, behold a vista from a high mountain, savor an exquisite meal, or delight in flashes of sunlight through a forest, you instinctively know what it's like to be transported from the mundane to the truly beautiful. And suddenly, life is filled with joy and satisfaction; you could even be suffering terribly yet feel life is worthwhile. God built beauty into our world as a testimony to his own loveliness, all so that we might experience him. Because God transcends the ordinary, he intends for beauty to do the same. Beautiful art and true science should point us to higher thoughts, nobler ambitions, and elevated affections. They should point us to Jesus.

Meditate: What are the beauties in your world that elevate your spirit?

88

A Tender Soul

When we are faithful to keep ourselves in
His holy Presence, and set Him always before us;
this not only hinders our offending Him, and doing anything
that may displease Him, at least wilfully, but it also
begets in us a holy freedom, and if I may so speak, a
familiarity with GOD, wherewith we ask, and that
successfully, the graces we stand in need of.

— Brother Lawrence, page 29

All it takes is a slight wind to set the thin, fragile leaves on our birch tree quivering. I want my soul to be like that. When the Spirit breezes my way and whispers, "If you binge-watch that show, it'll shrink your soul," I click the remote off. When the Spirit hints, "I see you replaying mental movies of your successes, and the pride is driving me away. Do you really want that?" I respond, "I do not!" I don't want to face the day having less of the Spirit of Jesus, less of his power and guidance and comfort in my life.

I crave *more* of him. I strive to make my soul responsive. I want to snap to attention when the Spirit speaks. I want a soul that immediately comes into alignment, sharply salutes, and declares, "Here I am, your servant; speak, Lord!" I yearn to be instant in obedience and absolute in my trust, not allowing little sins to wheedle their way in like "little foxes" that spoil my closeness with Christ (see Song of Songs 2:15). I pray, "Oh, Lord, save me from being spiritually sluggish or hardened by habitual sinning, unable to be nudged, prodded, or even pushed toward you." I want a tender soul. I may not be sinless, but I *can* sin less. With heaven's help, this can be you, too, as you win battles in small things. You are charged with the responsibility of keeping your soul wide open toward Christ. Intimacy with your God is at stake.

Meditate: It's worth anything to have
a pure and free heart, supple and
submissive to Jesus.

89

Abundant Gifts

I am filled with shame and confusion, when I reflect
on one hand upon the great favours which GOD
has done, and incessantly continues to do me; and on
the other, upon the ill use I have made of them, and my
small advancement in the way of perfection.

—*Brother Lawrence, page 50*

L et's suppose a man knocks on your door one morning and hands you one hundred dollars. He smiles and says there are no strings attached. The bill is simply a gift. You'd be bubbling over with thanks. Imagine your delight when he returns the next morning with another free hundred dollars. He keeps this up for a whole week, and you are speechless with gratitude.

Now, suppose he continues this routine for the next six months, each day giving you a fresh one-hundred-dollar bill. After so long a time, your appreciation might wane, as you have come to expect his gift, even rely on it. If the man is late, you could feel slightly irritated. Soon, you just place a note on the door: "Put my gift in the mailbox, please." Finally, after twelve months, the daily gifts stop. You look out your window, and much to your chagrin, you see the man now giving one-hundred-dollar gifts to your neighbor. *How dare he!* you think. *Where's my hundred dollars?* You feel slighted by the gift giver, and even resentful. "He built me up, only to let me down," you fume. And yet, how unreasonable it is to respond this way to generosity!

I must never take God's gifts for granted. Each morning when I sit up in my wheelchair, the first things I see through the bay window are our backyard roses and a birdbath. I see the tall silver oak trees by our fence and the Santa Monica mountains in the distance. Whether it's sunny or raining outside, it is all beautiful to behold. It is an abundantly generous gift that God hands me every day.

Meditate: Open your eyes to God's gifts today . . .
and rejoice in his many mercies.

90

This Cup

We ought to give ourselves up to GOD, with regard
both to things temporal and spiritual, and seek our
satisfaction only in the fulfilling of His will, whether
He lead us by suffering or by consolation,
for all would be equal to a soul truly resigned.

— Brother Lawrence, page 9

In Luke 22, we see Jesus in the Garden of Gethsemane in the early morning hours before his crucifixion. He is down on his hands and knees, heaving and groaning in horror. Already, he is staring into the undistilled evil churning in the cup he's about to drink. Trembling, he pleads, "Father, if you are willing, take this cup from me" (Luke 22:42). In other words, "Father, I am facing sheer hell here, so if there's any other path through this, I'd rather take it. Not the cross." But in the next breath, he adds, "Yet not my will, but yours be done." With those words, it was settled. Jesus considered obedience to God more important than a detour around Calvary.

I have my own small Gethsemane, as it were. I deal with chronic pain, and like my Savior, I often pray, "Lord, I am facing hell here, so I'm asking for you to take this cup of pain away from me." But, like Christ, I add that important qualifier, "Not my will, but yours be done."

The answer I hear most often is, "You must drink this cup." It's not the answer I hope for, but I willingly comply because I prize God's will above all else. If I were healed but separated from God, I would have nothing. Worse yet, I would be choosing to drink from a cup of evil, for nothing is more chilling than ignoring his will. There are more important things than living a pain-free life, and being wedged in the middle of God's will is one of them.

Meditate: Is there a difficult cup God has put before you? How will you respond?

91

Holy Grit

We ought to . . . *enliven our faith.* That it was lamentable
we have so little; and that instead of taking *faith* for the
rule of their conduct, men amused themselves with
trivial devotions, which changed daily.

— Brother Lawrence, page 8

I am a woman of faith. When I say that, I don't mean I am a person who only *mentally* assents to foundational doctrines about the Christian religion. If my faith meant only what I believe about Christ in my mind, it would not be faith at all. Faith in Christ will always stay in the world of theory and shadows, ambiguous and hazy, until it is called forth and put to the grind. Faith needs *exercise* so that when someone asks me, "Who is this Jesus, and what do you believe about him, Joni?" I can confidently respond, "He is my fountain of joy in all my sufferings, and let me prove that by the way I trust him."

Faith is just a word—a fancy, religious word—until it is put to work and scuffed up. Until it emerges from the work of life with a little holy grit on it. Far from ethereal, faith is "the substance of things hoped for, the evidence of things not seen" (Hebrews 11:1, KJV). Faith in Christ has substance; in other words, my faith is rock-solid proof of the appeal and power of Jesus Christ. My faith is also evidence of things I cannot see yet stake my very life on. I cannot see the better world Jesus has secured for me, but I set my heart on it; I lay up treasures there; I lift my prayers to his throne there; I await the new heavens and new earth, the resurrection of the dead, and the life of the world to come. To have great faith is to hunger greatly for our better country rather than settle for the passing pleasures of this life.

Meditate: How will you exercise
your faith today?

92

Strength to Endure

Take courage, offer Him your pains incessantly,
pray to Him for strength to endure them.
Above all, get a habit of entertaining yourself often
with GOD, and forget Him the least you can. Adore
Him in your infirmities, offer yourself to Him from
time to time; and in the height of your sufferings,
beseech Him humbly and affectionately (as a child his
father) to make you conformable to His holy will.

—Brother Lawrence, page 57

When you're in pain, Jesus feels the sting. He feels its knifing edge and the way it wilts your resolve. Jesus senses the urgency of your pain. To him, you are like the woman who tugged on the fringe of his garment—helpless and hurting and hemorrhaging human strength (see Luke 8:43–48). When your trembling need touches him, power goes out to you from his very essence. It is exactly the same as "the working of his great might that he worked in Christ when he raised him from the dead and seated him at his right hand in the heavenly places" (Ephesians 1:19–20, ESV). Christ's power infuses possibilities into utterly impossible situations. Even as impossible as your pain.

If God can raise the dead—and he does, without a doubt—he can raise you up out of the deathly despair of your pain. The incomparably great power of Christ is within your grasp. So draw close enough to Jesus to reach out and touch the hem of his garment. He will give you power. Power to endure, hold on to hope, and find courage. Power that'll see you through the worst of times. Power not so much to master your circumstances but to find your Master in them. Oh, friend, that your trembling hand can reach out and arrest God Almighty in his tracks should infuse your heart with courage.

Meditate: May the hem of Jesus's garment be your most cherished place of hope and healing today.

93

Together

I will pray for you; do you pray instantly for me,
who am yours in our LORD.

—Brother Lawrence, page 41

When Nehemiah was rebuilding the crumbled walls of Jerusalem, the workers were spread thinly along the perimeter of the city. They were easy targets for the enemy, so Nehemiah told them, "The work is very spread out, and we are widely separated from each other along the wall. When you hear the blast of the trumpet, rush to wherever it is sounding. Then our God will fight for us!" (Nehemiah 4:19–20, NLT).

There's your battle plan. Satan is hell-bent on frustrating, and even stopping, your work in Christ's kingdom. His tactic is to separate you from your praying friends; that way, his chances of taking you out are stronger. Don't let it happen. Do not go it alone, and do not feel embarrassed to confess your need to others. When I feel swamped by work, overwhelmed by pain, or spiritually lethargic, I know I'm vulnerable, so I sound the trumpet blast. Whether in a text, phone call, or email, I send out the word, "Help, I need prayer!"

When you are in anguish, experiencing discouragement, or feeling overwhelmed, lean on your warrior friends who, at your trumpet call, will come running with resources—a heartening word, intense intercession, a fitting Scripture, or the warmth of their presence. All of it conveys the strength of togetherness that God uses to fight for his people. "The LORD your God is in your midst, the Mighty One, will save" (Zephaniah 3:17, NKJV). Gladly ask Christian friends to bear your burden, for your mighty and merciful Savior always dispatches fresh supplies of strength and endurance.

Meditate: Are you under spiritual attack?
Drop everything and call a friend.

94

Loving the Cracks

GOD knoweth best what is needful for us,
and all that He does is for our good.

— Brother Lawrence, page 61

Kintsugi is a Japanese method for repairing broken pottery. Rather than conceal the lines of a fracture, the potter incorporates the crack into a beautiful new vessel in which all the broken places are visible and lovingly accented in gold. What was broken becomes a glorious work of art that treats the breakage as part of the history of the vessel rather than something to disguise or discard. "Golden joinery," as *kintsugi* is called, reflects the artful skill of the potter.[22]

God does *kintsugi* on his people all the time. When our lives are shattered by a terrible trial, he puts us back together in a way that does not disguise our injuries but incorporates them into our personal story of redemption. Our lives become richer and more attractive than they were before the trial—it's what redemption through Christ does. God has no intention of concealing your broken places; he displays his grace through them so others will admire the elegance of his *kintsugi* in your life. It's all for his glory and your good.

God is a masterful potter who enjoys redeeming broken things. And although a painful trial may not hold any promise of good at the time, God pledges to you,

> I will never stop doing good to them, and I will inspire them to fear me, so that they will never turn away from me. I will rejoice in doing them good and will assuredly [create a beautiful *kintsugi*] with all my heart and soul. (Jeremiah 32:40–41)

Meditate: Give him the broken pieces of your life.
He has something beautiful in mind.

95

One Remedy

When the mind, for want of being sufficiently
disciplined at our first engaging in devotion,
has contracted certain bad habits of wandering
and dissipation, they are difficult to overcome, and
commonly draw us, even against our wills, to the
things of the earth. I believe one remedy for
this is, to confess our faults, and to
humble ourselves before GOD.

— *Brother Lawrence, page 48*

Jesus taught one way of living over and over, saying, "Unless a kernel of wheat is planted in the soil and dies, it remains alone. But its death will produce many new kernels—a plentiful harvest of new lives" (John 12:24, NLT). The lesson is a hard one. Unless you allow Jesus to push you down deep into the dark soil of suffering, you will remain alone on the surface of life. Your tiny seed-self will stay hard, dry, unyielding, unproductive, and tossed about. Nothing of any eternal good will happen in you or through you.

But when you allow God to tenderly break you, things change. Your little seed-self dies. You become lowly, willing to descend into a dark place for as long as God desires. There, a wondrous transformation takes place. Planted in the will of God, your death to self produces an abundance of peace and joy in your heart, and God brings forth a plentiful harvest of transformed lives all around you.

It's one of Christ's principles: death produces life. Denying your heart of its wants and preferences leads to a rich spiritual life in Christ. You become the kind of person God uses powerfully in his kingdom. Praise God, he has transformed the dark soil of your suffering into a place of resurrection joy. This morning and throughout your day, purpose to die to self and rise to Jesus. It's the rhythm of a healthy spiritual life.

Meditate: We must die daily to self.
What does that look like for you today?

96

A Deeper Healing

God often sends diseases of the body,
to cure those of the soul. Comfort yourself with the
sovereign Physician both of soul and body.

—Brother Lawrence, page 55

Often Christians ask if they can pray for my healing. I always welcome the prayers of God's people, but after all is said and done, God has not raised me out of this wheelchair.

When people want to pray for a miracle, I'll offer them a list of specifics (this always gets them excited). I ask them to pray for a deeper healing than they might expect. I'll say, "Will you ask God to uproot my peevish attitude when things don't go as I wish? Ask God to deal with my spiritual laziness and selfishness. Ask him to convict me when I hog the spotlight, keep a record of other people's wrongs, or cherish inflated ideas of my own importance. Ask God to shame me when I say one thing but do another." By their expressions, I can tell they aren't expecting these sorts of "specifics."

Jesus has priorities, especially when it comes to physical healing. For the man who cured withered hands and blind eyes also said,

> If your hand . . . causes you to sin, cut it off and throw it away. . . . And if your eye causes you to sin, gouge it out and throw it away. It is better for you to enter life with one eye than to have two eyes and be thrown into the fire of hell" (Matthew 18:8–9, NIV84).

Jesus did not die to make us healthy but to make us holy. He came not to make us comfortable but to heal us of our propensity to sin. The best cures have to do with eschewing sin and drawing closer to Jesus Christ. It's better than any amount of walking.

Meditate: How might this devotional change the way you pray?

97

Grace and Gratitude

He requires no great matters of us; a little
remembrance of Him from time to time, a little adoration:
sometimes to pray for His grace, sometimes to
offer Him your sufferings, and sometimes to
return Him thanks for the favours He has given you,
and still gives you, in the midst of your troubles, and to
console yourself with Him the oftenest you can.

— Brother Lawrence, page 46

I cannot make my heart feel grateful. But there are times when I am lying in bed in miserable pain, I look up and, near tears, whisper, "God, I am so *happy*." How is that possible? I do not rejoice in my horrible pain. Far from it. I rejoice in the abundant outpouring of grace that God gives in response to that pain. He hears my plea, sees my yawning need, and fills it with grace that is commensurate to my pain; actually, since he's so generous, he fills my need to over-flowing. The result is that I am stunned and surprised by sheer happiness. My gratitude is in proportion to how much I need the grace of Jesus, and when I require him desperately, his grace virtually eclipses my physical agony.

I love this connection between grace and gratitude. Humanly speaking, I should not be happy when I'm lying in bed, stiff with pain, yet I can't stop thanking Jesus Christ for all that he has done for me.

Grace-inspired gratitude to God completely alters the face of my suffering. I know how strange it sounds, but there on my bed, I am free to go head-to-head with my affliction without anxiety or fear. I am not detached from pain; rather, I am engaged with it in a healthy way, knowing that I will never, ever plumb the depths of the reservoir of *grace* God has for me in suffering.

Meditate: Often, thanking God has nothing
to do with thankful feelings.

98

Out of the Grave

Useless thoughts spoil all: mischief begins there;
but we ought to reject them, as soon as we perceive
their impertinence to the matter in hand, or our salvation;
and return to our communion with GOD.

That at the beginning I had often passed my time
appointed for prayer, in rejecting wandering thoughts, and
falling back into them. That I could never regulate my
devotion by certain methods as some do. . . .

All bodily humiliations and other exercises are useless,
but as they serve to arrive at the union with
GOD by love. . . . I found it the shortest way to
go straight to God by a continual exercise of love,
and doing all things for His sake.

—Brother Lawrence, pages 14–15

We have gilded the real Savior with so much "dew on the roses" that many people lose touch with the earth-shaking facts of his resurrection. Only minutes before Mary Magdalene arrived at the tomb, the man was stiff, gray, and stone-cold dead. Suddenly, the lifeless corpse stirred, opened its eyes, rose from its slab, and as the grave mysteriously opened, walked out into the dark, cool garden night. If this weren't the gospel account, we'd think we were reading a scene from a horror novel. No wonder many of the people who first saw the resurrected Christ were frozen with fear—hours earlier, Jesus was a corpse; now, he is alive!

A syrupy picture of Jesus requires nothing from us; a nostalgic idea of him requires no conviction or commitment. It lacks power because it lacks truth. So for a moment, brush aside the birds and the lilies, and consider the facts: A dead man walked out of his grave. And as he did, this man, alive with God's glory permeating every fiber of his being, proved that he had conquered all the demonic forces of darkness. He had satisfied the wrath and judgment of God. He had defeated the last great enemy: death. The resurrection of Jesus became the first fruit of a bountiful harvest that will soon be reaped—the resurrection of all Christians. If you belong to him, you will one day receive a body like his, perfectly suited for heaven and earth—and this transitory world that you love so much will be like a candle compared to the sun.

Meditate: Plumb the depths of the Resurrection and your life will never be the same!

99

God's Good Purposes

Be satisfied with the condition in which GOD places you: however happy you may think me, I envy you in your current illnesses. Pains and sufferings would be a great paradise to me, while I should suffer with my GOD; and the greatest pleasures would be hell to me, if I could relish them without Him; all my consolation would be to suffer something for His sake.

—Brother Lawrence, page 56

The other day I read these sweeping words in Psalm 84:11: "No good thing does [God] withhold from those whose walk is blameless." It was such a profound promise that I decided to look up *good* in the dictionary. *Merriam-Webster* defines it as anything that is profitable, agreeable, advantageous, and pleasant. If we judge God by that definition, the good things he gives should always be agreeable and pleasant. "Obviously, they are not," says the woman who's lived a half century in a wheelchair!

God is not primarily concerned with our comfort and physical well-being. He cares about those things, but he is mostly concerned about the condition of our souls. So how do we read Psalm 84? If our walk is blameless, God will not withhold peace. He will not withhold virtue or faith or courage. He will not withhold grace when we come to him in need. We will be able to run spiritually and not grow weary; we'll be able to walk in faith and not faint (see Isaiah 40:31). He will not withhold opportunities to sow his seed or shine his light. He will not withhold patience or endurance or the favor of his nearness and sweetness. He will not withhold the gift of heaven-sent joy. None of these things will he withhold from those who walk uprightly.

Trust God when all seems hopeless, and he will make your soul brave and steadfast. If life seems unbearably hard right now, remember that some of God's best gifts must be unwrapped in the darkness. So believe that he is up to something good—the kind of good that will last for all of eternity.

Meditate: What "good thing" did the Lord slip
into your hands during a recent trial?

100

A Willing Vessel

In difficulties we need only have our pathway
back to JESUS CHRIST, and beg His grace,
with which everything becomes easy.

—Brother Lawrence, page 18

Ken has set up a computer desk where I can work next to our sliding glass door. When I need a break, I rest my eyes upon a plaque on our patio wall. Surrounded by potted plants, flowers, and a wren house, it reads: *So Very Thankful . . . Forever Grateful . . . Unbelievably Blessed.*

No matter how I feel, those words are always my pathway back to Jesus Christ. Everything is easy, as Brother Lawrence puts it, when I recognize that Jesus is an avalanche of help and hope. He is an abundance of power, peace, and joy. His Spirit rushes toward me in a whirling river of unending grace, always seeking the lowest point in my life and longing to fill me (as long as I see myself as empty). Jesus looks for the willing vessel, not the Christian who says, "Yes, the death and resurrection of Christ provide benefits to me, and as a believer, I'm in line to receive them." Rather, Jesus delights in the Christian who says, "Help, help me, Jesus. I'm empty; please fill me!"

I would not be that willing vessel were it not for my wheelchair. Just as water seeks to fill the lowest level, so grace looks to fill the lowliest believer. Hebrews 4:16 says, "Let us then with confidence draw near to the throne of grace, that we may receive mercy and find grace to help in time of need" (ESV). That's the point. Grace is for times of need. The needier you are, the greater your capacity for grace. The challenge for us is to constantly recognize our need. The wheelchair does this for me, so I am very thankful, forever grateful, and unbelievably blessed.

Meditate: Would you say you are so very thankful . . .
forever grateful . . . unbelievably blessed?

101

Home

If in this life we would enjoy the peace of paradise,
we must accustom ourselves to a familiar, humble,
affectionate conversation with Him: we must hinder our
spirits wandering from Him upon any occasion: we must
make our heart a spiritual temple, wherein to adore Him
incessantly: we must watch continually over ourselves,
that we may not do, nor say, nor think anything that
may displease Him. When our minds are thus employed
about GOD, suffering will become full of . . . consolation.

— Brother Lawrence, pages 60–61

I love how Brother Lawrence refers to our heart as a spiritual temple. My heart is where the Spirit of Jesus resides, so I want it to be a fitting and welcoming place for him. A place where Jesus feels at home, where he can wander into any chamber and find it clean and furnished to his liking. I want my heart to be his happy place.

When I read how the good kings in the Old Testament—Solomon, Hezekiah, and others—took great pains to consecrate and adorn the temple in Jerusalem, it's a picture of how I am to manage my own heart. Like the priests of old who were charged to fill the temple with only sanctified things (cleansed items set apart for worship), I am charged in the same way to fill my heart with "whatever is true, whatever is noble, whatever is right, whatever is pure, whatever is lovely, whatever is admirable" (Philippians 4:8). Like the Levites who sang of God's worthiness in the temple courts, you and I are "a royal priesthood . . . that you may declare the praises of him who called you out of darkness into his wonderful light" (1 Peter 2:9). I want my heart-temple to be a place of song and worship, of wonderful light where the Light of the World can shine, at home in delight and wondrous in joy.

Meditate: *Jesus loves living in a happy heart.*

102

The Grace to Work Well

So, likewise, in my business in the kitchen
(to which I naturally had a great aversion,) having
accustomed myself to do everything there for the love
of GOD, and with prayer, upon all occasions, for His grace
to do my work well, I found everything easy, during
fifteen years that I have been employed there.

— Brother Lawrence, page 13

Jesus was so weakened from his vicious flogging that he stumbled and sank under the weight of his own cross. So the soldiers pressed a passerby named Simon to carry it. And like that unsuspecting man in the crowd, we are passersby as well. We remain strangers, aloof to another's need, standing at a distance and politely observing . . . until God presses us into service.

You are perhaps a bystander who would not normally get involved, but your aunt is recovering from a stroke and needs help. Your neighbor just came home from the hospital and needs assistance. An acquaintance in your church was recently diagnosed with cancer and requires a hand with housework. Such ordinary needs do not seem like kingdom work, but if you sense even the slightest pressure to lend a hand, you can be certain it is the King who is pressing you into his service. All so that you, like Simon, might help a faltering stranger bear his cross. Yes, your plans will be interrupted, and you'll feel put upon, but when has normal Christian service ever *not* been sacrificial? When has cross bearing ever *not* come with pain, inconvenience, and cost? It's the nature of every act of Christian service, for when you lift the needs of others on your shoulders, it's like a cross—heavy, uncomfortable, and requiring much effort. So remember Colossians 3:24, for "it is the Lord Christ you are serving." The work is hard, but his grace is *yours*.

Meditate: Help bear a heavy cross on another's shoulder . . . you'll be serving like Simon.

103

The Roving Mind

You are not the only one that is troubled with
wandering thoughts. Our mind is extremely roving;
but as the will is mistress of all our faculties, she must recall
them, and carry them to GOD, as their last end.

—Brother Lawrence, page 48

S piritual warfare is a knock-down, drag-out fistfight with the devil, right? A noisy, tumultuous battle that wholly engages where our feet take us and what our hands reach for? Maybe not. Our fiercest fighting against the Enemy usually happens out of sight—on the battlefield of our minds. The war rages hot and heavy in solitary moments while lying on the beach, relaxing on the couch, or idly flipping through a magazine. In private moments, we can easily permit our thoughts to wander wherever they wish. Quickly (and naturally), they go south. A shocking image might pop into our heads, yet we are not quick to bring it into the light or shut it down. We reason that if we don't admit sinful thoughts, we cannot be held accountable: *What, me? I'm not doing anything wrong.* We are not fooling God; he knows our thoughts before we even think them (see Psalm 139:2).

We are ultimately shaped by what we *allow* our minds to feed on. When you are alone, be aware that indulgent, self-centered thinking will ultimately determine the future you. In those secret places, partner with the Holy Spirit and elevate your thoughts toward God and what pleases him. Cultivate an everyday righteousness so that your right thinking shapes you into who God wants you to be. The next time you are alone and struggling, please "be transformed by the renewing of your mind" (Romans 12:2). Go and do damage to the devil on the battlefield of your thoughts today!

Meditate: Right thinking makes for right living.
And it delights God.

104

Have Courage

I have told you that, He sometimes permits bodily diseases to cure the distempers of the soul. Have courage then: make a virtue of necessity: ask of GOD, not deliverance from your pains, but strength to bear resolutely, for the love of Him, all that He should please, and as long as He shall please.

— *Brother Lawrence, page 59*

Did Jesus die to give the good life to everyone with faith enough to grab it? You be the judge. Our Savior himself was poor, and most of the early Christians were too. James had his head cut off. Peter was imprisoned. Stephen was stoned. John died in exile on a barren island. Christians in Jerusalem were chased from their city. Peter described Christians all across Asia Minor as suffering "grief in all kinds of trials" (1 Peter 1:6). Many were slaves. Many were women with unbelieving husbands who didn't understand them. Many were singles filled with longing but afraid to marry due to the uncertain times. Many fell sick. Their property was confiscated. They felt the pull of temptation and knew the pain of a bruised conscience. All belonged to churches with real problems. All needed constant encouragement to keep going. Perhaps a page from Paul's diary says it best: "I have labored and toiled and have often gone without sleep; I have known hunger and thirst and have often gone without food; I have been cold and naked" (2 Corinthians 11:27).

In all this, these ancient believers were merely obeying their Savior who said, "If anyone wants to come after Me, he must deny himself, take up his cross daily, and follow Me" (Luke 9:23, NASB). Their godly response to suffering serves as an example to us (see 1 Corinthians 10:11). Oh, friend, look to the saints of old and be inspired. Follow their displays of bravery. Look to their lives when faced with your own hardships. Be valiant and have courage, for like them, "if we endure, we will also reign with [Jesus]" (2 Timothy 2:12).

Meditate: "For I am convinced that neither death nor life, neither angels nor demons, neither the present nor the future, nor any powers, neither height nor depth, nor anything else in all creation, will be able to separate us from the love of God that is in Christ Jesus our Lord" (Romans 8:38–39).

105

Life Is Not a Contract

I expected after the pleasant days GOD had given
me, I should have my turn of pain and suffering;
but that I was not uneasy about it, knowing very well,
that as I could do nothing of myself, GOD would not
fail to give me the strength to bear them.

—Brother Lawrence, page 11

When grappling with suffering, it is so easy to appeal to God on the basis of our performance. We've kept our noses clean, spoken up when others talked Jesus down, and been tracking well with prayer and Bible reading. Then we question why God hasn't dealt with us more equitably when the marriage proposal doesn't come or when the migraines keep getting worse. But following Jesus does not involve a pact, as if "I'll do such and such, and then God will be obliged do this and that (or something close to it)." When we subconsciously negotiate with Jesus, it reveals a sad misunderstanding of what it means to be born again.

The Christian life is not a contract. It's a death. His death *and* yours. When I gave my life to Jesus, it was that. . . . I gave it all: my comforts, safeties, individual rights, wants, and needs. I acquiesced control (as if I ever had it in the first place). So now when my pain fails to get better but instead worsens? I remember the terms of my salvation for "I have been crucified with Christ and I no longer live, but Christ lives in me. The life I now live in the body, I live by faith in the Son of God, who loved me and gave himself for me" (Galatians 2:20). Oh, the joy of dying to myself—my wants and preferences—that I might have King Jesus living his joy-filled, glorious life through me.

Meditate: He doesn't owe us a thing . . .
yet he gives us everything.

106

In Tranquility

Trouble and disquiet serve rather to distract
the mind, than to recollect it; the will must bring it
back in tranquillity; if you persevere in this
manner, GOD will have pity on you.

—Brother Lawrence, page 49

Scripture is filled with all sorts of metaphors for truth—lost coins, grains of wheat, houses on sand, hidden pearls, sheep that stray, and manna from heaven, to name a few. I've compiled several of my own metaphors, and I have a lively imagination that puts them to good use. When unruly thoughts trouble my mind, I whistle for my "sheepdog," imagining a border collie that's skilled in corralling wandering fantasies as though they were unruly sheep. I charge my sheepdog to herd those random feelings toward my Savior and "take captive every thought to make it obedient to Christ" (2 Corinthians 10:5).

My feelings and thoughts care nothing about the Bible, so my will is the border collie who snaps at their heels and drives them back to the path of righteousness. I grab my thoughts by the scruff of the neck; I push them into the pages of Scripture to give them a good dose of gospel truth. I show my idle thoughts who is the real boss of my soul, for I must not allow shiftless thinking to rule over me. I am like the psalmist who commanded his foolish musings, telling his soul, "Put your hope in God, for I will yet praise him, my Savior and my God" (Psalm 42:5). Practicing the presence of Jesus is just that—a practice. It is a "doing," a daily discipline. It is whistling for that border collie to drive every lazy thought to the foot of the cross where each idle tendency learns to submit.

Meditate: Sharpen your skill in corralling wayward thoughts.

107

Simple Prayers

We ought to act with GOD in the greatest simplicity,
speaking to Him frankly and plainly, and imploring
His assistance in our affairs, just as they happen.
That GOD never failed to grant my prayer one way
or another, as I have often experienced.

—Brother Lawrence, page 12

My friend was renting out a room in her house and wanted my help in processing the rental agreement. After ten minutes of filling in an electronic form, it struck me: "We haven't prayed!" Since it was only a simple form, I second-guessed the Spirit's prompting: "God has given us common sense for things like this. Let's not waste time but just plow ahead." Most would agree. "Fill in the blanks" do not require God's counsel, right? But should ease be the measure of whether or not we pray?

Since it was the Spirit who pricked me on such a simple matter, I decided he must have good reasons. Perhaps he wanted me to cultivate a lifestyle of prayer concerning mundane, everyday needs or acknowledge that there is never a good time *not* to seek the Lord.

Virtually all of Israel's sordid adulteries and wickedness traced back to a failure to inquire of the Lord and listen to his Word. Back in the time of Hosea, a refusal to consult God—even in the simplest matters—resulted in famine, drought, and God's displeasure. In our day, it will result in a drought-stricken soul. So my friend and I paused, pushed away from the computer, and bowed before God to ask his guidance. Just then, the Spirit urged us to pray about to whom the room should be rented (which was just as important as, if not more than, the easy-fill document). Always respond to the slightest promptings from God regarding the smallest of matters. Do not be hard of hearing when he beckons you to pray.

Meditate: Prayer is for the simple,
the frank, and the plain, and God
delights in our attention.

108

Bear Your Cross

Let us make way for grace; let us redeem the lost time, for perhaps we have but little left: death follows us close, let us be well prepared for it.

—Brother Lawrence, page 40

Long after my accident, when I drew closer to Christ, I was helped immensely by these brief words from Samuel Rutherford: "You cannot sneak quietly into heaven without a cross. Crosses form us into [the] image [of Jesus]."[23] From this, I learned two things: The path to heaven is much like the path to Calvary—mostly uphill, filled with danger, and stained with blood. Next, I learned that if I want to be like Jesus, I must bear a cross. I can't have Jesus without a cross. But it's not a one-size-fits-all cross that's generic to all; it is a cross specific to me. *My* cross. It's honed by God and heavy enough to ensure that I'll require his help every step of the way (it wouldn't be a cross if it were easily borne).

So when I daily pick up my cross, I "die *to* the sins that Christ died *for* on his cross."[24] I die to complaining, fears of the future, comparing my lot with others, and coddling doubts about God's character. My cross cuts at and carves away my sin; it wounds me and finally perfects in me the glorious image of my Savior. It's why the presence of Jesus is my dearest companion on the road to heaven. I love to fix my eyes on him who, for the joy set before him, endured his cross and sat down at the right hand of God's throne. And when I finally arrive at that throne? Lord willing, those last few miles will be the most fruitful, and I will have nothing else to do but gladly die.

Meditate: Does your cross feel too heavy?
Ask God's help in carrying it.

109

The Consolation of Suffering

The worst afflictions never appear intolerable, but
when we see them in the wrong light: when we see
them in the hand of GOD, Who dispenses them; when we
know that it is our loving FATHER, Who humbles and
distresses us, our sufferings will lose their bitterness, and
become even matter of consolation.

— Brother Lawrence, page 62

The beauty of being stripped down to nearly nothing is that God can then fill you with himself. Suffering doesn't teach us about ourselves like a textbook. Suffering is more like a sandblaster that grinds and obliterates the veneer on our characters. Suffering strips us of our facades, reaching down into where we do not want it to go, digging deep and exposing the true stuff of which we are made. Often, it's not very pretty. Although suffering leaves us exposed and sometimes shamed, its most worthy role is to empty us of ourselves.

It is our emptiness, not fullness, that God is after. For when sin, self-importance, and self-reliance are drained from our souls, we can then be better bonded to Christ. If we insist on knowing suffering's purpose, it's simply this: to know Jesus Christ better. To identify with *him* in *his* afflictions. To gain a greater understanding of the unthinkable price *he* paid for our salvation. True, suffering will do many good things for us—strengthen our faith and our characters and foster sensitivity toward others who hurt—but even our worst afflictions are mainly intended to draw us to Jesus. As deeply as suffering reveals things about you, it reveals more about the Savior you love. It will bring you into a new relationship with yourself, but mainly, it will bring you into a trusting place, a new relationship with God.

Meditate: *Our suffering is more about Jesus than us.*

Your All in All

I had been long troubled in mind from a certain belief that I should be damned; that all the men in the world could not have persuaded me to the contrary. . . . This trouble of mind had lasted four years; during which time I suffered much.

That since that time I have passed my life in perfect liberty and continual joy. That I placed my sins between me and GOD, as it were, to tell Him that I did not deserve His favours, but that GOD still continued to bestow them in abundance.

—Brother Lawrence, pages 10–11

When I gave myself to Christ, including my rights, needs, passions, and preferences, I embarked on a journey of losing myself for his sake. I agreed to behold him and adore him. I vowed to grow into the person that Jesus designed me to be, the person he imagined long before he laid the foundation of the world. That person is an image of himself; why wouldn't I desire to be like Jesus, the holy and righteous one? So I strive to change, go deeper, walk circumspectly, and obey. But in all my striving, I must ask, Am I indeed pursuing him and his holiness, or am I striving to impress him and thereby win his favor? Do I hope to "wow" him with my spiritual disciplines and holy habits? "Look at me, Lord! Aren't you delighted with me?"

It's something I must constantly guard against. For as we grow in Christ, we will not always experience the satisfying feeling of becoming more holy. Instead, in increasing measures, we will often possess an unsettling awareness of our sin. This is the strange side effect of sanctification. As you become more like Christ, you will feel less holy, not more holy. You will be struck by your unrighteousness, not your righteousness. The fact that you feel like a sinner—even the chief of all sinners—is a good sign that you're growing God's way. For when you fall facedown, realizing that Jesus is everything, he then becomes your all in all.

Meditate: What does it mean that Christ is your all in all? Pray it be so!

Thankful for These

I'm not your average writer. My hands are not able to tap computer keys, pull a book off the shelf, or highlight a paragraph for later research. Maybe other quadriplegics boast in their independence, but I'm not among them. I'm all about interdependence; I lean *hard* on others for help and am always saying thank you.

That brings me to the point of this page. Bear with me as I shower gratitude on the people—the dear friends—who made this book possible.

I love how Paul Pastor jumped on the idea for *The Practice of the Presence of Jesus*. From the start, he and his team grasped the vision for the content and design and thought nothing of working overtime to make this modest book sing.

My dear friend Andrew Wolgemuth of Wolgemuth & Associates does far more than represent me, his author. Over the years, he has been a springboard for ideas, an avid intercessor, and my go-to guy for anything to do with books. Thank you, Andrew, for your patience and prayers.

Now, back to hands that don't work: I am grateful to my typist friends who sit across from me and scramble to keep up with my flow of words. Whenever Kathren Martinez,

Francie Lorey, or Lisa Miehl paused in the manuscript to say, "*That* really spoke to me," I knew I was on track. Even my husband, Ken Tada, chipped in.

But Catherine Cobb did more than type. She works as communications manager at Joni and Friends, but she doubles as my copy editor, research assistant, contract analyst, and format specialist. *The Practice of the Presence of Jesus* would still be a book proposal were it not for her extraordinary skill and expertise. I also "robbed" Emily Mayfield from our Communications Department to polish whatever Catherine put on her desk. Meredith Hinds worked on John Sloan's end, researching, writing, and scrambling to keep up with him—*thank you,* Meredith.

Most of all, I am indebted to my precious friend and long-time associate in publishing, John Sloan. I first met this remarkable man in 1983 when he served as executive editor at Zondervan—I was on my third book with the company and soaking up everything I could from the experts. And John was the undisputed expert in all things publishing, marketing, and writing. He has been my tireless advocate since the beginning and is the one who came up with the idea for *The Practice of the Presence of Jesus*. His name really should be in bigger type on the cover, for I do not admire anyone more in the book world than John.

Saving the best for last, I praise my Savior, Jesus Christ, for blessing me with the joy of writing about his majesty and matchless grace. I thrive on practicing his presence, and for nearly fifty years he has blessed me with innumerable ways of telling others about him. Perhaps he thinks I have something to say since I have long depended on him in my wheelchair. Whatever his reasons, I love writing about him. I'm sure Brother Lawrence felt the same. And so, I pray every reader will meet Jesus in a fresh way in this humble book.

Notes

1. Direct quotes in this section are taken from Brother Lawrence, *The Practice of the Presence of God* (London: J. Masters & Co., 1896), 36, 32, 42–43, 14, 62, 43 (in order of appearance). For the historical details in this section about Brother Lawrence, the following sources were consulted: Brother Lawrence, *The Practice of the Presence of God* (Peabody, Mass.: Hendrickson, 2004); Kathleen Mulhern, "A Medieval Mystic Untimely Born?," Christian History Institute, https://christianhistoryinstitute.org/magazine/article /lawrence-a-medieval-mystic-untimely-born; "Brother Lawrence of the Resurrection (1614–1691)," Boston Carmel, https://carmelitesofboston.org/history/our-carmelite -saints/brother-lawrence-of-the-resurrection; "Brother Lawrence: Practitioner of God's Presence," *Christianity Today Online,* www.christianitytoday.com/history/people /innertravelers/brother-lawrence.html; Gary Thomas, "Brother Lawrence," Closer to Christ. Closer to Others., https://garythomas.com/resources/free-resources/brother -lawrence.
2. Edward Mote, "My Hope Is Built on Nothing Less," Hymnary.org, https://hymnary.org/text/my_hope_is_built_on _nothing_less.

3. Jonathan Edwards, *Heaven: A World of Love* (Pensacola, Fla.: Chapel Library, 1998), 11.

4. *Book of Common Prayer* (New York: Seabury Press, 1979), 331.

5. "Napoleon Crowned Emperor of France," The Cultural Experience, December 6, 2018, www.theculturalexperience.com/news/napoleon-crowned-emperor-of-france.

6. Alexander MacLaren, "Expositions of Holy Scripture," Bible Hub, https://biblehub.com/commentaries/maclaren/psalms/34.htm.

7. Charles Spurgeon, "January 9th—Evening Reading," Blue Letter Bible, www.blueletterbible.org/devotionals.

8. Joni Eareckson Tada, *Songs of Suffering: 25 Hymns and Devotions for Weary Souls,* (Wheaton, Ill.: Crossway, 2022), 102–3.

9. Mary Ann Baker, "Peace! Be Still!," Hymnary.org, https://hymnary.org/text/master_the_tempest_is_raging.

10. Thomas Brooks, *The Complete Works of Thomas Brooks,* vol. 5 (Charlottesville: University of Virginia, 1867), 210.

11. Charles Wesley, "And Can It Be That I Should Gain?," hymnal.net, www.hymnal.net/en/hymn/h/296.

12. George D. Watson, *Soul Food* (Cincinnati: M. W. Knapp, 1896), 39.

13. John Ford, "God's Glory Alone" (sermon, Church in the Canyon, Calabasas, Calif., August 27, 2017).

14. Robert Robinson, "Come, Thou Fount of Every Blessing," Hymnary.org, https://hymnary.org/text/come_thou_fount_of_every_blessing.

15. Charles Spurgeon, "March 4th—Morning Reading," Blue Letter Bible, www.blueletterbible.org/devotionals.

16. James Smith, *The Believer's Daily Remembrancer* (Cambridge, Mass.: Harvard University, 1864), 341.

17. Tada, *Songs of Suffering,* 18–19.

18. *The New Testament of Our Lord and Savior Jesus Christ*

(Philadelphia: American Baptist Publication Society, 1865), 398, 1 Timothy 1:11.

19. Amy Carmichael, *Things as They Are: Mission Work in Southern India* (New York: Young People's Missionary Movement, 1906), 158.

20. Richard Baxter, *The Saints' Everlasting Rest,* abr. Tim Cooper (Wheaton, Ill.: Crossway, 2022), 137, 69–70.

21. Charles Spurgeon, "Rare Fruit," The Spurgeon Center, www.spurgeon.org/resource-library/sermons/rare-fruit.

22. Kelly Richman-Abdou, "Kintsugi: The Centuries-Old Art of Repairing Broken Pottery with Gold," My Modern Met, March 5, 2022, https://mymodernmet.com/kintsugi-kintsukuroi.

23. "Quotes by Samuel Rutherford," Bukrate, https://bukrate.com/author/samuel-rutherford.

24. Tada, *Songs of Suffering,* 108.

About Joni's Ministry

The heart of Joni Eareckson Tada leans toward the millions of people around the world who struggle with disabilities. Their families live in poverty, pain, and despair. It's why Joni began Joni and Friends in 1979. The organization is committed to bringing the gospel and practical resources to people living with disability around the globe. For decades, the ministry has been transforming people's understanding of disability in the community and in the church.

Joni and Friends accomplishes this through an array of programs, including domestic and international Family Retreats, Marriage Getaways, and Warrior Getaways. Wheels for the World has delivered more than two hundred thousand wheelchairs and Bibles. Joni's Houses are centers in developing nations that serve the spiritual and practical needs of people with disabling conditions. The organization provides respite programs as well as internships for a new generation of young people who are passionate about serving Jesus among families with special needs.

A disability can take many shapes and sizes—whether it is grief, a deep sense of loss, pain, or an invisible chronic condition, Joni and Friends wants to share hope in your hardship. No matter what the limitation, if you have been touched by the insights in this book, or if you need help or prayer support, let us know how we may serve you. Contact us here:

response@joniandfriends.org

Joni and Friends
PO Box 3333
Agoura Hills, CA 91376
(818) 707-5664

joniandfriends.org

About the Authors

A diving accident left JONI EARECKSON TADA a quadriplegic at seventeen years old. She emerged from rehabilitation with a determination to help others in similar situations. In 1979, she founded Joni and Friends, a ministry committed to showcasing the gospel to people living with disability. Joni is the author of forty-five books and lives in California with her husband, Ken.

JOHN SLOAN is a writer and editor living in Colorado Springs. He has served as Joni Eareckson Tada's editor for more than two decades. John enjoys writing about people from other centuries and loves reading to his grandchildren about any century.

About Joni's Art

Although Joni is a quadriplegic, she learned to draw while holding pens and brushes between her teeth. The line drawings in this volume were rendered over a period of twenty years. For more information about Joni and her artwork, please visit joniandfriends.org.

About the Type

This book was set in Sabon, a typeface designed by the well-known German typographer Jan Tschichold (1902–74). Sabon's design is based upon the original letter forms of sixteenth-century French type designer Claude Garamond and was created specifically to be used for three sources: foundry type for hand composition, Linotype, and Monotype. Tschichold named his typeface for the famous Frankfurt typefounder Jacques Sabon (c. 1520–80).